T0208546

UNITE THE USA
Discover the ABCs of Patriotism

Stacie Ruth and Carrie Beth Stoelting

WESTBOW
PRESS
A DIVISION OF THOMAS NELSON

WestBow Press books may be ordered through booksellers or by contacting:

WestBow Press
A Division of Thomas Nelson
1663 Liberty Drive
Bloomington, IN 47403
www.westbowpress.com
1 (866) 928-1240

Because of the dynamic nature of the Internet, any web addresses or links contained in this book may have changed since publication and may no longer be valid. The views expressed in this work are solely those of the author and do not necessarily reflect the views of the publisher, and the publisher hereby disclaims any responsibility for them.

Any people depicted in stock imagery provided by Thinkstock are models, and such images are being used for illustrative purposes only. Certain stock imagery © Thinkstock.

Scripture taken from the New King James Version. Copyright 1979, 1980, 1982 by Thomas Nelson, inc. Used by permission. All rights reserved.

Scripture quotations are from The Holy Bible, English Standard Version® (ESV®), copyright © 2001 by Crossway, a publishing ministry of Good News Publishers. Used by permission. All rights reserved.

Scripture quotations taken from the Holy Bible, New Living Translation, copyright 1996, 2004. Used by permission of Tyndale House Publishers, Inc., Wheaton, Illinois 60189. All rights reserved.

Scripture taken from the Amplified Bible, Copyright © 1954, 1958, 1962, 1964, 1965, 1987 by The Lockman Foundation. Used by permission.

ISBN: 978-1-4908-1354-7 (sc)
ISBN: 978-1-4908-1355-4 (hc)
ISBN: 978-1-4908-1353-0 (e)
Library of Congress Control Number: 2013919021

Printed in the United States of America.

WestBow Press rev. date: 11/25/2013

Dedication

We dedicate this to heroes (a.k.a. veterans) and their families –especially families whose loved ones never came home from war. We pray for you. May you know God, His comfort, and His love to the fullest.

We dedicate it to our parents, and in memory of our grandparents. They deserve recognition as unsung but inspiring, hard-working American patriots who encouraged our love of God and country.

Most of all, we dedicate this book to our Lord, who is the ultimate <u>Freedom-Giver</u> for all who trust in Him.

"For freedom Christ has set us free..."-Galatians 5:1 (ESV)

"And what more shall I say? For the time would fail me to tell of [the prophets] who through faith subdued kingdoms, worked righteousness, obtained promises, stopped the mouths of lions." --Hebrews 11:32-33 (NKJV)

Contents

Preface

"Freedom is never more than one generation away from extinction.
We didn't pass it to our children in the bloodstream.
It must be fought for, protected, and handed on for them to do the same."
–Ronald Reagan

As members of the post-9/11 generation, we find ourselves particularly awakened to the fact that time is short and action is needed. So we prayerfully and optimistically started a uniting, inspiring movement: UnitetheUSA.org. With thousands of members across the country, **Unite the USA** exists to promote positive patriotism and to encourage conservative standards. We honor veterans, give a voice to the poor and afflicted, and to inspire people to fully apply "in God we trust" to daily life. As a Christian web site, <u>Unite the USA</u> encourages Americans to unite in the fight for our rights –especially Christian rights. We hope to activate the post-9/11 generation to become positive patriots of faith! Consequently, we decided to write this book and entitle it the same as our movement.

Love God and neighbor. That's what we need in America today. We need to return to the basics. We need to unite the USA to pray and fight for what's right. ASAP. Hence, you hold this book in hand.

<u>Reality</u>: A killing poison of apathy courses through the veins of our country's eagle. She's still flying, but her wings burn from fatigue. Her wings look almost normal, but the reality threatens: She could fall unless we rise to pray and work for her return to greatness.

You see, America's moral debt exceeds that of our national debt. In a nutshell, here's what we mean: Disinviting God invites immorality. Immorality invites apathy. Apathy invites anarchy. Anarchy allows for autocracy. And autocracy annihilates a country.

Yes, we're at war. It's invisible, and highly divisible. It's a spiritual war. This is about good vs. evil. It's about the moral conditions and overall health of our nation.

We may shock you. You may dismiss us as "alarmists" or make fun of us. But we'll tell you the truth anyway because *we care too much not to share*: America must wake up or else she will suffer a wound worse than 9/11/01. A self-formed storm so cataclysmic, a suicidal attack so fatal could take down our gorgeous country. The battle rages –whether you look or not. And the war includes you –whether you like it or not.

If Americans called on the Name of Jesus instead of using His Name as a swear word, our country would be a lot better off. We need good, Christian common sense. Some people recline in a comfortable state of denial. Surrounding them are clutters of thoughts justifying inaction, acceptance of wrongs, etc. They don't want to hear the truth. It means change... But it also means freedom! So tell the truth anyway. It's more than worth temporary discomfort to grasp and then hoist high the torch of freedom! As the Lord said in John 8:31-32, "If you abide in my word, you are truly my disciples, and you will know the truth, and the truth will set you free."

As the founders of Unite the USA, we are prayerfully working hard to inspire the American people -who are the heart of our country- to be active, informed citizens. Each month, our online magazine features articles by people like Phyllis Schlafly, Star Parker, and Rick Santorum, includes action points, and provides resources. Sign up for our online monthly magazine at www.UnitetheUSA.org. With this book and our site, you can learn how to change America and return her to her roots of freedom, faith, and family.

In this book, we fail the politically correct test. Repeatedly. With that said, we don't share with a vendetta. We share with love for God and man. In these pages, we share everything with love for God and country and do not shy from sharing what we sincerely believe will change America from death to life.

Today, when headlines and difficulties discourage us, remember there is hope in Christ and there is hope for America. Never stop fighting for justice and freedom. We are *still* one nation under God. Join us as we unite the USA in a fight for our eagle's return to greatness. May our book inspire you to do your part to defend and preserve America – and help her soar again.

To begin, let's recite the pledge:

"I pledge allegiance to the Flag
Of the United States of America,
And to the Republic for which it stands:
One Nation under God, indivisible,
with Liberty and Justice for all."

American Trivia: Did you know that the pledge of allegiance was written by a Baptist minister? Learn more about it at this link: http://conservapedia.com/Pledge_of_Allegiance (The Star Spangled Banner, 2011).

PART I:

America's Heroes and You:
How to Appreciate Veterans and Country

CHAPTER ONE

"Is This What We Fought For?"

"Greater love has no one than this, that someone lay down his life for his friends." –Jesus Christ, as quoted in **John 15:13 (ESV)**

A personal story

May 11 never escapes our notice. We shared about it on Fox News. And it influences our lives to this day. On that day in 2007, my sister and I traveled down a familiar Iowa road wrapped by a beautiful blue sky. (As two young college students, we anticipated summer break.) Since Mother's Day quickly approached, we had decided to bring our grandma her gifts early. We were traveling west on good old HWY 3. We were on our way to Grandma's. That's all.

Suddenly, a motorcyclist and car crashed at full-speed. I saw it all. (Out of respect for the family, we refrain from sharing details about the violence.)

I called 911.

Carrie and I rushed to the victim and prayed with him, putting faith in Christ. He passed away before any authorities arrived. But we knew that he, having had faith in Jesus, was in Heaven. (Do you know you'd go to Heaven if you had that accident happen to you? You don't have to wonder. You can know you'll go to Heaven when you die. Visit the back of the book to learn how to know God personally, too.)

Post-Accident Effects

Carrie and I will never forget it. We'd been patriotic and Christian before "the accident", as we commonly call it. But we'd never be the same: Since that time, we've more boldly (yet respectfully) shared about our faith in Jesus and we've treasured our veterans and troops even more. You see, they have seen far worse violence than we did. They deserve our utmost respect and support. That's why we sing and share nationwide about the Lord and our country. We meet many heroes (a.k.a. veterans) at events. At one Veterans Day event, we met "Frank"...

"Is this what we fought for?" the elderly man's voice quivered. His bloodshot blue eyes revealed a heart for America and complete disappointment with Washington, D.C. He hated to see the anti-God, anti-freedom policies fading the fabric of our flag. He shifted his cane from one hand to the other while bracing himself against the wall so that he could still stand tall.

Frank had fought in WWII and always attended the Veterans Day event in his region. As the speakers and singers for the event, my sister, Carrie, and I felt our hearts melt inside. *What could two Iowan young people say to a hero who fought so that our freedoms could stay?*

Carrie and I looked at the hero and then sent a sisterly glance to each other. Oh, yes. We knew each other's thoughts: *God, please help us say the right thing. Amen.*

"We thank God for you, Frank. You are a hero. And we want you to know that we're going to do everything we can to fight for freedom on the home front."

After the event, the elderly man's words echoed in our minds throughout the days ahead: *Is this what we fought for? Is this what we fought for? Is this what we fought for?* Since that time, we've continued to regroup and renew as we seek to serve God and country –in spite of America's current challenges.

The time has come not to fold up shop. The time has come to fold our hands. America's problems don't overwhelm God. But He cannot condone our killing of His creation (abortion), etc. America must repent and turn to God instead of rejecting Him and then asking His blessing. He is good. He is holy. He is true. He loves each of us and desires each of us to repent and turn to Him. May the loving Lord Jesus be welcomed in the hearts of many Americans this year and in the years ahead. We must seek God and set goals under His direction– not merely a party's selection.

The goal must not be popularity. The goal must not be espousing what is PC (politically correct). The goal must be in loving God and fellow man in the face of false accusations in our nation. God bless each citizen who grasps God's hand and says to Him, 'Yes, Lord. Together, we can!'"

> **"Before any great achievement,
> some measure of depression is very usual."**
> **—Charles Spurgeon**

Today, depression looms over our beautiful land: According to the Center for Disease Control, depression now afflicts 1 in 10 Americans[1] and continues to rise in number. Our country suffers from a moral decline, depression incline, and rejection of the divine. It's time to turn to God.

So why do our "hope in God" Facebook posts often become "shared" and "liked" by thousands of people across the United States? Well, to be honest, we don't know. We're not famous. We're simply two sisters in Iowa who know what we and all Americans need: Hope

---

1   (2011). *An Estimated 1 in 10 U.S. Adults Report Depression.* Atlanta: Centers for Disease Control and Prevention. Retrieved February 19, 2013, from http://www.cdc.gov/features/dsdepression/

in God. Pure and simple. When we hope in God and follow Him, good things follow...like appreciating what's important. (That's why we give musical tributes and programs to honor veterans, who are important.)

It's Important to Appreciate Veterans.

Sadly too often, the media and Hollywood ignore troop recognition and veteran appreciation. We believe it's time to unite and honor our troops. For instant inspiration and increased appreciation, consider the ultimate sacrifice by Navy SEAL Mike Monsoor:

Navy SEAL Mike Monsoor and his two teammates climbed to rooftop positions during a firefight in Ramadi, a Sunni insurgent stronghold west of Baghdad. Suddenly, an insurgent grenade bounced off Monsoor's chest. It landed on the roof.

Monsoor looked at it. He had two choices: escape and live yet watch his two comrades die or die in their place. We'll let President Bush's speech reveal what happened as he quoted one of the survivors:

"'Mikey looked death in the face that day and said, 'You cannot take my brothers. I will go in there instead.' In that terrible moment, he had two options –to save himself, or to save his friends. For Mike, this was no choice at all. He threw himself onto the grenade and absorbed the blast with his body."

He chose to stay. They lived. He died. He died for his comrades, but -ultimately- he died for his country.

Countless men and women like Mike Monsoor have willingly given their very lives for us. Over 1,343,812 brave Americans have died in military service. There have been over 1,145,523 wounded and 38,159 MIAs. (Numbers updated regularly. Please refer to current statistics for accuracy.)

Clearly, freedom is not free –it comes at a high price. But, the men and women who willingly served their country knew very well that they may not return home yet they still boldly served. Throughout

American history, the U.S. military has ensured and protected freedom. In our own country, a strong defense has kept our country the land of the free for over 200 years.

Honor the memory of those who have given their lives to keep us free. Thank our veterans and current servicemen and women for their hard work and tireless efforts to protect freedom. Our heroes know that freedom is worth it. They've seen tyranny and the consequential pain and disparity. That further emboldens them to fight for freedom. They're heroes. Period.

One such hero was fellow Iowan Glenn "Mac" McDole: In 1940, McDole enlisted in the U.S. Marine Corps. On August 12, 1942, he bravely entered the Palawan prison camp in the Philippines. Two long years later on December 14, 1944, Japanese soldiers slaughtered about 93% of American POWs. The Japanese lied. They announced false air raids to move prisoners into underground shelters. Then, they mercilessly poured gasoline on top of them and used dynamite and machineguns to murder the POWs. Our brave soldiers were slain by evil, blood-thirsty hands. They died a hellish death for our freedom. Yet McDole escaped.

Amazingly, Glenn McDole was one of eleven young men who escaped. He was the last man out of the Palawan Prison Camp 10A. McDole and the ten other survivors dug into refuse piles, hid in coral caves, and slogged through jungles and swamps to safety. The horrifying conditions suffered by McDole and his comrades were endured for America's freedom. Our freedom. *Your freedom.*

During World War II, Japan captured thousands of American soldiers like McDole as prisoners of war (POWs). They were held captive in camps from Burma to the Philippines. The Japanese treated all captives with the same disdain: starvation, disease, beatings, torture, and even execution.

Clearly, POWs such as Glenn McDole strongly value freedom. They know from experience what it is like to live in bondage. They know firsthand what it is like not to be free.

Carrie and Stacie Stoelting with Col. Bud Day

As proud Americans, we're also proud of Col. George "Bud" Day, a native from Sioux City, Iowa. He was a retired U.S. Air Force Colonel and Command Pilot who served during the Vietnam War. His years of service include five years and seven months as a Prisoner of War in North Vietnam. He was the most decorated U.S. service member since General Douglas MacArthur. Col. Day received some seventy decorations, with a majority for actions in combat. In addition, Col. Day was a recipient of the Medal of Honor and the Air Force Cross.

Yes, Col. Day was a remarkable man and one of America's greatest heroes. We had the great honor of meeting him and singing for him –an experience we will always treasure. Col. Day deeply loved his country and freedom. He solidly believed in the U.S. Constitution and freedom. (But Col. Day would have been the first to tell you that complete freedom comes from knowing Jesus Christ Who set us free from sin and death.)

Yes, we live in the land of the free because of the brave. God bless our veterans and our servicemen and women! God uses regular people like all of us. So it's important to be active in sharing God's blessings with our veterans. The following seven points are for you to apply and share on social media (and in everyday conservation):

7 Ways to Encourage Military Appreciation

1. **When a soldier dies, stop saying, "For what?" The answer is . . . *for you*!** For us to stay free, they pledged their lives. Not one of our troops who paid the ultimate price died in vain!

2. **Fight for our warriors by voting.** A rumor of today is that not voting is an option. Don't believe it. If you don't vote, you dishonor our fallen heroes. They fought and died for you to stay free. Research, pray, and VOTE. It's the American way!

3. **Tell kids over and over: Each one fought for you and me to stay free.** Citizens must unite and fight for what's right for our military.

4. **Twitter about the fallen heroes. Post pictures of the fallen heroes on Facebook.** (We provide such tribute pictures on our Facebook page.)

5. **Write a Letter to the Editor to remind people to honor and pray for our troops.**

6. **Show your veteran appreciation! Use the format of your choice –wear pins that remind others to pray for our military or use Pinterest.**

7. **Show your support and appreciation to our servicemen and women and send a care package.** It means so much to them to receive something from home. So, get busy and reach out to a hero today. Make it a family project. Here are some tips to send a care package.

The "How to" Guide for Care Packages:

1. **Shop for a variety of items such as nonperishable food and snacks like sunflower seeds, beef jerky, hard candy, gum and snack crackers.** Useful items like toothpaste,

hand lotion, wet wipes, hand sanitizer, shampoo, chapstick, and bath soap are always appreciated. Also include CDs, DVDs, magazines, small games, note pads and pens. If you are preparing a care package for a loved one, include photos, family videos, handwritten letters and copies of the local newspaper.

2. **Follow the restrictions established for military care packages.** Do not send perishable foods or candies that melt. Alcohol, firearms, and any time of weapon are not allowed in care packages. Do not send any product that may be considered harmful such as an aerosol spray can.

3. **Use the guidelines established for the care package itself.** The package cannot weigh more than 70 pounds. The box or container that is sent must be no more than 130 inches total combined girth and length. The completed care package needs to be sent by way of the United States Postal System by "Priority Mail." If not sent by Priority Mail, the package will take 8 weeks or even longer if mailed during the holiday mailing period.

4. **Be sure that you have the correct military address** to mail your care package because the package will pass through the Military Post Office (MPO) to be processed to the correct military base or location.

5. **Work together with military families in the same unit as your loved one** to make sure that all the members of the unit have care packages arriving from home. Ask the home front Commanding Officer or the assigned contact to stay updated about the military unit's location. Talk to organizations in your community about doing service projects for various military units that may not have a lot of home front support.

CHAPTER TWO

How to Become the Next "Greatest Generation"

"Success is not final, failure is not fatal: it is
the courage to continue that counts."
--Winston Churchill

"Rosie the Riveter." A 1940's image instantly comes to mind: The red bandana, strong arm, and determined expression instantly inspire us. A strong woman working hard for America. A strong woman who didn't shirk work because she needed more "me time". A strong, intelligent woman who walked and talked her beliefs about God and country. A strong woman who didn't disrespect men. As two young women from Iowa, we like Rosie.

Fast-forward to today: While flying to Washington, D.C., we visited with a fellow passenger who was young, fair-haired, and from rural America –in those regards, quite similar to us. Then she opened her mouth:

"So what's the name of our First Lady?"

We thought she was joking. She chewed some gum, threw her hair back, and stared at us with big blue eyes. Our eyes widened: She was serious. We answered her and left the conversation with more questions. How did our generation get this way?

"Sara" (who follows our music and mission, www.UnitetheUSA. org) jumped into a conversation with me. She's a waitress, and "Sara" had something to say that further alarmed us about our generation's desperation for education and inspiration to do the right thing in our country:

"Susan just told me she didn't even know what a Congressman was," the waitress shrugged. "I guess she never learned. So I told her. She seemed really interested."

I (Stacie) felt my eyes bug a little bit. But I quickly recovered and enthusiastically replied, "Way to go for telling her! I wish more people would be so willing to step up and share about our country. Good for you!"

But, after the conversation, I felt sick at heart about our country's rampant apathy: Apathy fells many a country. This cannot be ignored.

Stacie and Carrie on Fox News

Fox News labeled us "leaders of the post-9/11 generation" during one of our interviews in NYC. We feel surprised and blessed by such distinctions, but we're really just two young Iowan women who love America, sing our hearts out, and pray hard.

So how do we do something? Plenty of people write books and talk their heads off yet never put their feet on the pavement. It's time for positive patriots to stand up. But first, we must embrace a game plan. Let's copy the Greatest Generation.

12 Ways to Copy the Greatest Generation

1. **Interview members of the Greatest Generation while there's time.** Ask your church to recommend someone for you to visit. Ask your librarian. Or e-mail a nursing home. Ask them what they did. Personal testimonies will educate and inspire you more than you can envision.

2. **Pray. The Greatest Generation embraced prayer and prayed regularly –including during government-led events and broadcasts.** Get involved with a good prayer group in your church community. For additional prayer, we have a prayer group online. It's called "Praying Pals" because we pray each Friday for a list of prayer requests – including for our country, troops, leaders, etc. Join us at www. PrayingPals.org.

3. **Be resourceful** – The Greatest Generation would reuse their resources. They were the original recyclers. For example, our grandparents saved certain plastic bags (i.e. bread bags) and used them for other items (i.e. to cover brownies).

4. **Respect our military.** Fly a flag. Visit wounded veterans. Contribute to pro-veteran organizations.

5. **Parents –not government- must parent America's children.** Teach kids why America is great!

6. **Try making something instead of buying it.** Example: Try

baking bread for fun. Even if it doesn't turn out perfectly, you'll appreciate bread so much more.

7. **Go to church regularly and take its message out with you to your community.** Invite a friend along and ride together for fun.

8. **Have regular family get-togethers with extended family, if possible.** Play patriotic music in the background once in a while.

9. **Write handwritten letters to loved ones.** And tell them you love them.

10. **Live without activities that take away from family time.** And instead enjoy every day life as a family –not just on weekends. Live it up with your family and friends! Invite your neighbors over. Do chores together instead of apart, if possible. Guard family time. Embrace God-given life today and hope for tomorrow!

11. **Honor the elderly instead of viewing them as extras.** Encourage kids to respect the elderly and include your elderly loved ones/friends as often as possible. Ask them to share lessons they've learned.

12. **Instead of reading a self-help book use the time to help somebody else in your neighborhood.**

Now that we've put down the Greatest Generation's foundation of faith, family, and freedom, we'll dive into some issues that warrant explanation and patriot activation. In other words, we'll help you get your mental rifles loaded!

"Duty is ours; results are God's." –John Quincy Adams

CHAPTER THREE

How to Value the Invaluable: Veterans

"Americans never quit." –**General Douglas MacArthur**

Recently, we experienced a tremendously inspiring event honoring a veteran. Was it in Washington, D.C.? No. Was it in a large arena? No. Was it one of the best events at which we've sung? Yes.

It was Colonel Elizabeth Johnson's retirement ceremony.

For 30 years, Colonel Elizabeth Johnson served valiantly in Iraq and other locations in the world. She did what so many people in the military do: saved lives, honored God, and made her country proud. "I enjoy helping people and being a source of comfort," she said.

Colonel Johnson witnessed the worst of war. Critically injured soldiers arrived near-death and Colonel Johnson provided the best care possible. Her capable hands tended to the needs of the severely injured –including amputations. Even during the most intense war-torn circumstances, Colonel Johnson stood prepared and ready to give our wounded heroes the best medical attention in her power. She was always on the job. And she saw it all.

Colonel Johnson traveled the world healing the sick and helping the healthy stay that way. Through the course of her military career,

Colonel Johnson's assignments included: Medical/Surgical clinical staff nurse (Fort Eustis, VA), operating room clinical staff nurse (Tripler Army Medical Center), Head Nurse, Operating Room, 47th Combat Support Hospital (Fort Lewis, WA), staff development coordinator (Operating Room, Madigan Army Medical Center), Director, Perioperative Nursing Program (Madigan Army Medical Center), Chief Perioperative Nursing (121 General Hospital, Seol, Korea), Chief, Perioperative Nursing Section (West Point), Chief, Perioperative Nursing Service (Landstuhl Regional Medical Center, Germany), Assistant Deputy Commander for Nursing (Fort Belvoir, VA), Chief, Perioperative Nursing Section (Walter Reed Medical Center), Deputy Commander/Deputy Commander for Nursing (14th Combat Support Hospital, Fort Benning, GA), and Commander (Fox Army Health Center, Redstone Arsenal, AL). In 1983, Colonel Johnson was deployed to Honduras in support of Ahas Tara II. Then in 2009, she was deployed to Iraq as Deputy Commander for Nursing, TF 14 MED in support of Detainee Healthcare Operations.

Colonel Johnson's military awards and decorations include the Bronze Star Medal, Meritorious Service Medal (with five Oak Leaf Clusters), Joint Service Commendation Medal, Army Commendation Medal (with two Oak Leaf Clusters), Army Achievement Medal (with one Oak Leaf Cluster), and the Expert Field Medical Badge. She is a member of the Order of Military Medical Merit and received the 9A Proficiency Designator. Clearly, Colonel Johnson is a remarkable woman and she is an extraordinary leader. It is impossible to fully express the gratitude Americans should feel for heroes like Colonel Johnson.

Read her own words:

> "What a privilege I've had to care for members of the military and their families. It was an honor to serve this great nation during both times of peace and time of war. During my 30 year Army career, I had the opportunity to provide nursing care for members of

the military from World War I and forward. All whom I met had a tremendous attitude of selfless service of which I readily witnessed with the OEF/OIF wounded warriors. I recall not one who wasn't more concerned for members of his/her unit more than self. I always fill with great pride and admiration whenever I think about my compassionate staff and the wonderful care they provided to all. Many thanks to all who pray for the safe keeping and healing of all who serve. A special thanks to Carrie Beth and Stacie Ruth for the graciousness they have for the military and their families. God bless you."

Of course, we appreciate her kind words and, most of all, we appreciate her. Meanwhile, we also have other veterans who are much older but whose golden, heroic virtue never fades. Many of our truly elderly veterans experience a lot of challenges and go unnoticed: While frail veterans shuffle down gray hallways of nursing homes, Veterans Day gets lost in the shuffle of fluorescent, fast-paced modernity. Following the trend each year, Election Day snatches attention from the already neglected Veterans Day. A personal story illustrates this fact:

With passion, Stacie sang the National Anthem for President George W. Bush. Near Election Day, the event attracted over 11,000 people –including the internationally famous. Thousands of people fused into a flowing mass and the crowd roared like a turbulent tidal wave. (It reminded us of the coliseum scene from Ben Hur.)

Before Stacie sang her heart out, she verbalized her heart to the audience and dedicated the singing of the National Anthem to her family, friends, and Jesus Christ. She also dedicated it to our President and members of the military.

For whom did the crowd cheer the loudest? For Jesus Christ? No. For our veterans? No. For the President? Yes. The President received the most deafening, passionate praises.

Recently, another presidential occasion eclipsed an event of vast significance: the homecoming celebration for the return of local missionaries, who have spent years of toil in Albania. The missionaries' homecoming occurred on the very evening and in the very town of the President's arrival. Who received more attention? The President did, of course. Sadly, such responses echo the imperfect message of the world: Riches, connections, offices and fame seem to win and dominate this world's game.

But our Heavenly Father rights all wrong! His eyes tenderly, lovingly view all of His children with equality. In fact, our Heavenly Father loves the President just as much as He loves the resident of a nursing home. He wants us to express His love to all –including veterans.

Most of us consider ourselves appreciative of veterans. We have them stand up in church. We pray for them. Yet do we think that we cannot locate blank squares on our daily planners to honor them with our time? Well, if so, we must expeditiously adjust our attitude about this issue: We need to focus on the fact that many veterans' hourglasses hold little sand on top.

It is urgent: Droves (especially veterans of World War II) die each day. Indeed, we must serve our servicemen soon. It is Biblical.

For further proof of our point's validity, consider God's command: "Render to all men their dues. [Pay] taxes to whom taxes are due, revenue to whom revenue is due, respect to whom respect is due, and honor to whom honor is due" (Romans 13:7, AMP).

We propose several simple ideas about how to honor our veterans. Pick one or more and discover eternal value in validating the invaluable veterans of our nation:

1. **Send a thank-you card or e-mail a caring note to a veteran in your life.** Or, if you don't know a veteran, contact a local care facility and inquire. You could send a card addressed to all veterans at a nursing home. Many nursing homes/ hospitals offer to deliver e-mails to residents. (Of course,

cards are more colorful and inspirational than e-mails. But e-mails are far better than nothing!)

2. **Call a veteran and thank him/her for serving.** Often, a short call sheds lasting light onto a veteran's soul. Many feel forgotten. We can flip that fact inside out!

3. **Send flowers.** We know this sounds morbid, but there is truth to this: Rather than wait for the funeral, we need to send the flowers now. Plus, they do not have to be big bouquets.

4. **Visit a veteran. Or take a veteran out to dinner.** Following their initial return home from war, many haven't savored a special meal given in honor of their service.

5. **Don't forget our young veterans.** They deserve an e-card, note, or gift, too. Our courageous college-age young men and women face countless challenges. Our efforts can combat depression induced by combat. Web sites such as www.amillionthanks.org serve as extremely easy media through which to convey thanks to our valorous veterans.

After we obey God's command to honor the deserving, we'll eventually experience the fulfillment of John 6:38 (AMP): "Give, and [gifts] will be given to you; good measure, pressed down, shaken together, and running over, will they pour into [the pouch formed by] the bosom [of your robe and used as a bag]. For with the measure you deal out [with the measure you use when you confer benefits on others], it will be measured back to you."

Let's take time to value the invaluable!

CHAPTER FOUR:

Veterans Fought for Your Right to Vote:
Voting is not an option. It's a must.

"Nobody will ever deprive the American people of the right to vote
except the American people themselves
and the only way they could do this is by not voting."
–Franklin D. Roosevelt

"Nah, I'm not voting," the self-confident man put his hands behind his head. "There's no point. My first choice didn't make it. And now the two main guys aren't too different. Both career politicians. I won't vote for a person who doesn't believe exactly like I do. It's a matter of principle."

Rewind! What's the problem with the preceding paragraph? The person dismisses apathy on a faulty concept of what voting should be: Voting is simply selecting the person who most parallels with your values. You won't find a twin of yourself whom you can elect. Let's knock out some of the key excuses for not voting:

- "I'm too busy." (**You can vote absentee.**)

- "My one vote doesn't count." (**One vote does make a difference! Some elections are decided by a handful of votes.**)
- I'm just not into politics. (**If you're an American citizen, you owe it to your country which allows you to live free.**)

Apathy shocks us. Why? It doesn't mean we're some sort of perfect patriots. Instead, we realize the cost paid with the blood of our soldiers. How can we not appreciate that for which our brave soldiers gave their lives?

Some people blame the young. But it's not our fault. Our generation and those following us are simply taught by the previous generations. It's time for us to stop trying to figure out why and start reaching out to young voters with respect and educating them with patience and kindness. Here's a story to illustrate this point:

Flying to D.C. to sing again, we visited with a young passenger. As a high school senior, she had been selected to represent students in her state. She conversed with us at rapid-fire speed. Suddenly, we started talking U.S. History. We started to talk about loving various aspects of our country's history...but she didn't know what we were talking about. She needed us to explain the basics. So we told her some exciting facts about our country's formation and government. She didn't know U.S. History, but she wanted to learn. (Just like most public schools, her school had apparently excluded U.S. History in its curricula.) But, sadly, many people simply don't care.

Over 1 million Americans cast votes...for "Dancing with the Stars." Yet millions of people toss aside their right to vote for leaders who could control their lives.

Let's get this straight: **Not voting is still voting.** Not voting empowers an extreme minority to rule a majority. Think about it: If you don't express your preference, you welcome deference

**Carrie and Stacie with Senator Chuck Grassley
at a town hall meeting. Senator Grassley visits
all 99 counties of Iowa every year.**

We aren't perfect, but we do try to vote every chance we get. And we've been thankful to sing for voters and leaders alike. It's exciting to celebrate our U.S. History and make history! At history-changing events, we have sung patriotic Christian songs for conservative luminaries ranging from the most-decorated veterans (like Col. Bud Day) to national leaders like Mike Huckabee, Rick Santorum, Chuck Grassley, and Steve King. In other words, we deeply desire to help establish Godly leadership...one vote at a time! It's pretty clear: We're pumped for patriotic action in America. Are you?

ACTION POINTS: This time, consider the V.O.T.E.R. points:

1. View the country from an eagle's eye and not from a feelings-only, close-range perspective. If we don't risk telling the truth to uninformed and/or misguided people, we risk hurting our country. Do it respectfully, kindly, and prayerfully. Put aside

temporary feelings of discomfort as you share facts about your candidate. The foundations of our country are at stake!

2. **Overcome apathy.** An active minority overtakes an inactive majority. Today, apathy runs rampant. Some Christians snivel, cross their arms, and refuse to cast votes for less than ideal candidates. "Why vote when my first choice didn't make it?" People depend on others to stand up for their values. Yet, if everyone thought that way, no one would stand and the country would fall.

   • Research the candidates. Who is pro-life, pro-elderly, and pro-small government? Learn more about candidates and their stances.

   • Employ the "friendly, firm, and fair" logic when conveying why you want other people to vote for your candidate.

   • Pray before you vote. Then pray for fellow voters. And pray for all candidates -even those of the opposition. (Changed hearts equal changed votes.)

   • Put up signs in your yard, on Facebook and Twitter, on your car, etc. And actually talk about it. (Again, fear of getting unfriendly responses only increases our country's chances to fall and fail.)

3. **Temper your temper.** Discover the effective results of rational, educational discussion. Be above dirty politics. Stay calm and respectful when in a challenging discussion. You will stand out.

4. **Energize people in your life.** Positive, respectful persuasion quickly ripples thru a nation until it builds into a wave!

5. **Refuse fear.** Silent conservatives, let's emerge from shyness and politely, positively vocalize truth. Frankly, a fear of hurting feelings hurts our country.

Apathy felled Rome. So stand up for Biblical values in America, your home. Don't discount the value of your vote when the votes are counted.

"Vote." Yes, it's a four-letter word. And so is "love." **If you love America, you'll vote.** It's that simple. Vote pro-life, pro-elderly, and pro-limited government!

By the way, we eventually heard from the high school senior. We're hopeful that she's heading in the right direction. Remember: If we pray and obey, God hears and draws near. Let's do that every opportunity we get. Let's vote!

CHAPTER FIVE

Hope and Truth about American Exceptionalism

"A troubled and afflicted mankind looks to us, pleading for
us to keep our rendezvous with destiny; that we will uphold
the principles of self-reliance, self-discipline, morality,
and, above all, responsible liberty for every individual
that we will become that shining city on a hill."
–Ronald Reagan

America shines as exceptional because her intent is to give honor
and responsibility to the individual –not the state. Unlike many
other countries, our nation never established a state religion, feudal
system, landed estates or hereditary nobility. America truly stands
as a unique beacon of freedom: a place where people live free of
government control. A sanctuary for families. *An oasis of freedom
for the oppressed.*

Beginning with the Puritans who arrived on the Mayflower
and continuing to the colonists of the 1700s, America was founded
by people who wanted to be free. (They especially sought religious
liberty.) Thomas Paine's book, *Common Sense*, stated that America
was a new country of nearly unlimited potential and opportunity

that had outgrown the British mother country. As a republic, the United States offered citizens freedom. Americans could live their lives without government dictating their every move.

Some describe this remarkable achievement as "American Exceptionalism" –a term developed in 1831 by Alexis de Tocqueville, a famous French visitor to America who wrote *Democracy in America.* De Tocqueville said, "The position of the Americans is quite exceptional, and it may be believed that no democratic people will ever be placed in a similar one."

Later, President Thomas Jefferson envisioned America to become the world's great "empire of liberty". He identified his nation as a beacon to the world and as a model for democracy and republicanism. Embracing ideals have allowed America to achieve higher goals and shine hope –like a city on a hill.

For most countries, family position determines those who have wealth and opportunities. However, in America anyone from any background can become educated or "climb the ladder of success" regardless of circumstances of birth and social rank. This aspiration is commonly called living the "American dream". Thanks to the First Amendment in the U.S. Constitution, Americans receive the five freedoms of religion, speech, press, assembly, and petition.

Reality check: In many countries, governments harshly and violently punish individuals who stray from the state religion. For example, China, Sudan, Saudi Arabia, Iran, and other Middle Eastern countries are intolerant of religious freedom –especially Christianity—and they punish those who disobey. But, in America, we have religious liberty: a gift we must protect.

People from around the world seek refuge here to escape Marxism, Communism, and other tyrannical governments. America has come to the aid of struggling nations so that they, too, can live in freedom. (Contrary to the liberal message, other countries do cherish Americans who helped them!)

Sadly, in recent times, certain leaders have flipped the opposite direction: American exceptionalism has been under attack: In

April 2009, President Barack Obama said, "I believe in American exceptionalism, just as I suspect that the Brits believe in British exceptionalism and the Greeks believe in Greek exceptionalism." This attitude strikes a sour chord: It's akin to Iowa State University fans being lukewarm and claiming that the University of Iowa thinks of itself as being just as exceptional and, therefore, they have the same worth. Or if fans of the New York Yankees would say that the Minnesota Twins had the same level of pride and support from their fans and, therefore, the same worth.

Yes, it's normal for countries to embrace their own national pride and should be encouraged –just like schools have school pride and sports teams have team spirit. But certain teams don't play well in the field. When people like President Barack Obama diminish our country's exceptional and winning position in the world, it is unacceptable. Unfortunately, good, old-fashioned Americanism faces internal enemies:

Without fail, the liberal media make statements that undermine our country's history, uniqueness, and importance. Even government leaders seem lackluster about the stars and stripes. As defenders of freedom, we believe that Americans must work hard to protect our country from internal attack.

Our history of freedom and stability isn't perfect (i.e. slavery and the Civil War), but it's the **best** in history: America still stands out from other countries: No other country has enjoyed such a record of unhindered individual freedoms.

In fact, during the small time frame in the early days of America, France experienced fifteen separate governments. Other countries have had a series of governments as well. For example, Brazil has had seven since 1822; Poland has had seven since 1921, and Russia has had four since 1918. And, the same is true for many other nations throughout Europe, Africa, South America, and the rest of the world.

The fact of our freedoms rests on the mercy of God and, as such, they should be cause for appreciative humility. We believe in

American exceptionalism -not prideful superiority. God has blessed and watched over America and we thank Him for those blessings.

We must remember that it is God who grants the grace, yet a nation must seek His face. He's the ultimate Judge (Psalm 75:7).

We must turn to God, humble ourselves, and realize the treasure which is America. God-given rights must be preserved. America deserves appreciation and prayer. Psalm 47:8 (NLT) states it clearly and concisely: "God reigns above the nations, sitting on his holy throne." God has used America to help many achieve the previously impossible!

As a conclusion, the words of President Ronald Reagan are perfect to share, "Freedom is never more than one generation away from extinction. We didn't pass it to our children in the bloodstream. It must be fought for, protected, and handed on for them to do the same."

>>>**ACTION POINTS:** We especially encourage that you buy and wear patriotic, tasteful clothing and accessories. Give them as gifts. We find that many Christian stores have good sales on patriotic t-shirts, etc. Go ahead! Show your patriotism! America IS exceptional! Please see the "+101 Take Action Now" resource in the back.

CHAPTER SIX

Never Give Up

"If we don't stand up and cry out now, we'll
sit down and cry about it later."
— **Stacie and Carrie Stoelting**

On December 3, 2012, Sgt. Jason M. Swindle's[2] widow gave birth to their child. *A boy.* Jason, Jr., was born on his late-father's 25th birthday. "I prayed about it. But there was no planning whatsoever. This baby had a mind of its own from the beginning," Chelsey explained. It's true: Jason, Jr. arrived unexpectedly on his heroic late-father's birthday.

Here's a bit of a background about this precious baby's late-father: You see, Sgt. Jason M. Swindle died for you. He died, yet little media attention showed it. Within two weeks, jihadists killed eleven Americans...nine of whom were American troops (a.k.a. heroes). Most media primarily featured Election 2012 instead. But we'll feature him:

---

2   Read more about this brave family here: http://www.fox16.com/news/story/Beebe-Army-wife-delivers-son-after-husbands-death/49AkvAiGh0ykeJJljxN0EQ.cspx.

Sgt. Jason M. Swindle loved his country and he paid for it with his life.

This strong, auburn-haired man from Arkansas never returned to his beloved, pregnant wife, Chelsey, and toddling son. And, when Chelsey gave birth, he wasn't there to hold their precious baby. (Pray for them, please.)

A soldier's sacrifice is also a family's sacrifice. Our hearts break for the families of these heroes... We must unite and honor their fallen loved ones while we increase prayer for the heartbroken families! Everyday such brave Americans fight (without Hollywood accolades). Yet U.S. citizens can change this. We can make them feel appreciated. Outreach is not out of our reach: Anyone can do something! Here's a great example:

CWA (Concerned Women for America) includes an excellent leader doing great things with the resources God has given her: Tamara Scott, with femininity and fervor, fights to bring our fallen heroes honor. Each year, in an Iowa church, a Veterans Day event commences to give tribute where tribute is due. The well-loved event is not given enough publicity by the press, and could (and should!) be standing room only. (That's our opinion.) The point of the matter is that it is up to each of us to spread the word and do what we can for this great land.

With the media misappropriating priorities, it's up to us, fellow citizens. **If we don't stand up and cry out now, we'll sit down and cry about it later.** Too many people risked their lives to arrive on this country's shore, worked hard for this country, fought for this country, and died for this country. How dare Americans of today get "burned-out"! That's just part of battle: It gets hot sometimes, yet God helps you fight in His way and in His time.

Instead of catching that awful patriotic "burn-out" after disappointment, let the fire build! Build the fire for truth and a return to freedom, faith, and family values! Let the fire spread across this gorgeous country! Turn from the wrong and return to the right. Let God lead you...and not polls. Fight to return to America's roots of freedom! And never, ever quit. The Founders fought the "Establishment" and taxes galore. Today, to the enemies of America within and without, we say, "No more!" Most of all, we invite God back. Fight for what's right! And never, never, NEVER quit!

The takeover of "anything goes" continues: Families sever. Kids kill themselves. Doctors kill unborn Americans. The elderly are not encouraged to live but to "die with dignity" in a form of passive euthanasia. Homosexual "marriage" entered common conversation. Yet true marriage (between a man and a woman before God) gets attacked by "no-fault" divorces, which has been known to be misused to the family's harm.

Where is God? Actually, the real question could be asked by God: America, where are you? Without question, this will ruffle the fragile feathers of those who desire to make the United States a refuge for humanism, socialism, nihilism, Communism, extreme feminism, and the overall umbrella of social Darwinism. As the dictionary defines, social Darwinism is: "a sociological theory that sociocultural advance is the product of intergroup conflict and competition and the socially elite classes (as those possessing wealth and power) possess biological superiority in the struggle for existence." (Example: Radical feminists embrace social Darwinism in that they believe females deserve help to overtake the unfair evolutionary gains of males. This has led to an exodus for moms from the home. Read more in *The Flipside of Feminism* by Phyllis Schlafly and Suzanne Venker.)

Yes, many of today's problems stem from the core of unbelief combined with social Darwinism. Here are some startling facts:

How the Moral Deficit of America Exploded

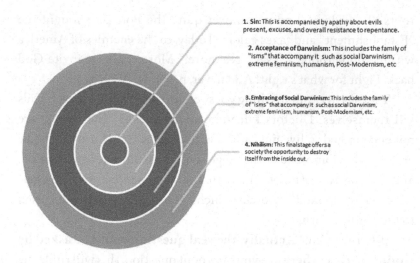

1. Sin: This is accompanied by apathy about evils present, excuses, and overall resistance to repentance.

2. Acceptance of Darwinism: This includes the family of "isms" that accompany it such as social Darwinism, extreme feminism, humanism, Post-Modernism, etc

3. Embracing of Social Darwinism: This includes the family of "isms" that accompany it such as social Darwinism, extreme feminism, humanism, Post-Modernism, etc.

4. Nihilism: This final stage offers a society the opportunity to destroy itself from the inside out.

(Graph of the Moral Deficit of America)

Nihilism results after Darwinism parasitically conquers education in a nation. The Encarta Dictionary's definition for nihilism speaks volumes:

ni·hil·ism (noun):
1. **total rejection of social mores**
2. the general rejection of established social conventions and beliefs, especially of morality and religion
3. **belief that nothing is worthwhile**
4. a belief that life is pointless and human values are worthless
5. **disbelief in objective truth**
6. the belief that there is no objective basis for truth
7. **belief in destruction of authority**
8. the belief that all established authority is corrupt and must be destroyed in order to rebuild a just society

Unfortunately, the educational system embraced an atheistic,

humanistic worldview. The truth of the matter is that we went wrong when we started saying everyone is right. Good and evil exist. To counter humanism, we propose a theory entitled, "Creator-Creation Theory": When young people experience constant interaction with loving adults who help them appreciate and follow their loving Creator, they assimilate Biblical truths in different ways at different stages of development (as made known by Jean Piaget) whereby the full person (spiritual, mental, behavioral, social) flourishes with faith in Christ at all stages of life. Apart from such an environment, bad conduct goes excused as "whatever works for you" and escalates until it permeates all cohorts of society.

When psychologists Abraham Maslow and Carl Rogers developed a popular concept of humanism, they sent a message that absorbed into America's faith-based and familial fibers: People are basically good, do not need a Savior, and should expect the best of everyone.

This excused sin as being unnecessary to address in the same way. Churches began diluting messages to appeal to the new culture's taste for unchained pleasure as humans celebrated their innate goodness. Unfortunately, feeding self-esteem and promoting positive messages to children ignored behavioral issues and allowed for sin to be accepted, discipline to be forsaken, and new confidence to be formed in a faulty god: good human beings.

The fact of the matter is this: Only with God can human beings do great things. When big projects are done apart from Him, pride bloats into a blinding, destructive component called narcissism. **Take a quick look at the contrast of statements made by two educational leaders approximately 200 years apart.**

Compare/Contrast of American Education Leaders:

BEFORE: "The Bible... should be read in our schools in preference to all other books because it contains the greatest portion of that kind of knowledge which is

calculated to produce private and public happiness."[3]
- **Benjamin Rush** *(Father of Public Schools Under the Constitution"; Signer of the Declaration of Independence; Surgeon General of the Continental Army)*

NOW: Education Secretary Arne Duncan has said, "Hopefully, someday we can track children from preschool to high school and from high school to college and college to career."[4] He has also said in a television interview that he unequivocally supports gay marriage. When asked if he thinks gay couples should be able to legally marry, he said: "Yes, I do."[5]

It boils down to this: Extreme liberals think they deserve to make your children theirs because they believe that the government can parent better than you. It's because they believe that we're not accountable to God and that we're innately good. But school shootings, bullying, Plan B (abortion in a pill form) filling high school vending machines, teen suicides, and other depravities prove otherwise. Indeed, when schools tossed out the Golden Rule, they invited trouble to rule. It's evident that children today crave love and direction, which only God can provide.

Interestingly, in liberal extremists' opinions, tolerance covers every people group...except Christians. Yet true Christians love God and neighbor. Liberal extremists (who still have a glimmer of conscience) find that their faint, gnawing conscience irritates them

3   Benjamin Rush, Essays, Literary, Moral & Philosophical (Philadelphia: Thomas & Samuel F. Bradford, 1798), pp. 94, 100, "A Defence of the Use of the Bible as a School Book."

4   Learn more about this dangerous governmental interference and indoctrination in the lives of children in our nation: http://www.wallbuilderslive.com/download/CommonCoreQuickFacts.pdf.

5   Read more: http://www.foxnews.com/politics/2012/05/07/obama-cabinet-member-duncan-backs-gay-marriage-one-day-after-biden-comments/#ixzz1uCvVNlkv

and they mislabel the blame for their irritation and deem Christians to be irritating. The truth is that they find the cross to be a stumbling block...an irritation to their quest for sins to be accepted in our nation. Pray for liberal extremists to know Jesus personally...to know His love and share it. Pray for revival in our churches. Pray for revival in ourselves...for true repentance and acceptance of God's ways instead of our own. Pray. And do not stay silent.

Silence during unacceptable governmental interference only equips the opponents of freedom. The time to speak and stand up is now or else later will not come. Keep sharing the truth and hoisting the torch of freedom in our great land! Share posts on Facebook so that others understand. Respectfully interact with your representatives in government and be persistent. They may get sick of it, but stick to it. Persistence combined with prayer creates positive change!

In summary, our country needs to return to Christ and the Constitution. Period. Be a part of getting our country to that point. With God, you can make a big difference!

>>>**ACTION POINT**: Pray for and support families with children in school. If you're a parent, prayerfully consider homeschooling or sending your children to a Christian school. If that's not an option, supplement your child's education with conservative materials that teach the whole perspective –not just the liberal one. (Also see the Resource section.)

PART II

America: *Yesterday's Mistakes
and Today's Heartaches*

CHAPTER SEVEN

Learn from the Past to Fight for Today's Families

"If we fail to solve this moral and spiritual crisis
we may be doomed like the great nations
of the past." –**Billy Graham**

Our prayer outreach, PrayingPals.org, receives hundreds upon hundreds of prayer requests each year. Most of them involve tragic family dysfunction and loss: suicides, arrests of prodigal children, affairs, divorces, drug addictions, etc. The requests are then prayed over by the prayer group. Encouragingly, thousands of people have joined PrayingPals.org to pray for all submitted prayer requests (as a whole). Praise reports continue to remind us that God continues to heal hearts and families. No wound exceeds His ability to heal. This fact holds great significance as families face tough times.

Today, unlike any other time in human history, families suffer. Marriages end. Children feel scared. In America today, the divorce statistics remind us constantly of the challenge and strain on American couples and families. Yet few people speak out openly about a very real contributing factor: In reality, the problems can often be traced to feminism, which has wreaked havoc on societal structure and, of course, the family unit. In the following paragraphs, both the problem and the answers to overcome such issues will be addressed in order to help families and couples in their pursuit of successful, Christ-centered marriages full of love and respect.

Today, relationships everywhere suffer the results of the cultural departure from solid, Biblical values in the home. In the face of extreme feminism, a jarbled message of what constitutes a successful family and marriage continues to pervade society. Entertainment, curricula, and even Hallmark cards often convey a strangely similar message: While men are worthy of mockery, women are unworthy unless promiscuously dressed or societally powerful. In part, the blame rests on social Darwinism.

As touched on in a previous chapter, social Darwinism invaded the landscape of upper-class society and academia in the late nineteenth century. Academic circles began to further embrace humanistic beliefs instead of Christian values. According to the online Merriam-Webster Dictionary, the term "social Darwinism" first appeared in usage in 1887 and the definition of it included that it was "an extension of Darwinism to social phenomena; specifically: a sociological theory that sociocultural advance is the product of intergroup conflict and competition..." (Merriam-Webster, 2013). That "intergroup" included extreme feminists who blamed the males for all afflictions of the less evolved yet deserving females of the human race. In essence, they believed that men had oppressed them and women needed freedom to overcome the patriarchal society.

Such social Darwinist beliefs included that men (who had the most wealth) appeared to be "the fittest" and women appeared to have been kept from advancing socially, financially, educationally, and politically (i.e. suffrage). Granted, social ills certainly existed for centuries prior to the advancement of social Darwinism and feminism. Rest assuredly, women's rights to vote and own property should have been granted to them far sooner. Yet the general disrespect of men and the transformation of women into power-hungry people who have used sexual attraction to get their way only disintegrated the overall benefits of voting and owning property.

However, the social Darwinists blamed men solely for oppressing women from overall advancement. Adherents to this social theory believed that women should "catch up" to men and that men were essentially the enemy. Competition between the sexes only heated and accelerated society's decline into deeper distrust and discontentment. The family suffered:

As the effects of evolution and associated theories like social Darwinism, the Biblical values of love and respect began to be shelved –much to the harm of family units. The lies of feminism purported that men had used religion to hinder women's biological and social advancement. People like Margaret Sanger, who founded the abortion-promoting organization now called Planned Parenthood, attested that the birthing of so many children and the burdens of homemaking only dulled the female sex. Consider her disturbing quote: "Birth control is the first important step woman must take toward the goal of her freedom. It is the first step she must take to be man's equal. It is the first step they must both take toward human emancipation" (Sanger, 1918).

With such mentality being integrated into society, more women leaders emerged with each new decade of the twentieth century, becoming more radical with each decade. As a whole, depression and anxiety for women only increased in comparison. Society (including marriage) declined enormously. For women growing up in the 1960's and 1970's, the messages of extreme feminism taught girls at an early age to detest the patriarchal system and fight back to be emancipated women. For example, in her book *Girls Gone Wise in a World Gone Wild*, Mary Kassian conveyed her era of the 1960's and 1970's in a succinct and distinct manner worthy of quotation: "Feminism taught the girls of my generation that men had terribly oppressed our mothers and grandmothers, and their mothers and grandmothers before them... Men had seized all the positions of power." (Kassian, Girls Gone Wise, 2010, p. 55)

The Feminist Movement's Momentum

Indeed, in the 1960's and beyond, technological and overall communication tools advanced and, with such tools as TV and the Internet, the feminist messages continued to snowball into each ensuing decade. As a result, women entered marriages with a built-in fear of male dominance. After all, women had learned from feminists that women were like previously enslaved minorities who needed liberation from the tyrancy of men. Instead of looking at the Bible (with proper hermeneutics), they turned to fight this fear with rebellion: They burned bras. They fought to add to the U.S. Constitution the Equal Rights Amendment, a proposed amendment that claimed to guarantee equal rights for women. However, in reality, it would have been bad for women and their families. Thankfully, conservative women like Phyllis Schlafly fought against it and won (Schlafly & Venker, 2011). Clearly, a cultural war against men existed in which women unknowingly also fought against themselves and their families.

Stacie and Carrie with Phyllis Schlafly

Unfortunately, many women believed a one-sided, misguided worldview. They did not know the truth: Contrary to feminist teachings, a mixture of both corrupt men and women shaped the cultural landscape. Yes, women certainly deserved to vote, own property, etc. But women could not make all men an enemy without also hurting themselves –as well as their marriages and families— in the process. This harsh reality seemed too obvious to be noticed by certain intellectuals of the twentieth century.

Consequently, in the 1990's, a myth that it takes a village (instead of the male-dominated family) was promoted. Conservative Christians were often mocked for not being as progressive. Yet the fact remains that Christians (often called "conservatives" in the political realm) and their families –not villages—must form the bedrock of a healthy society. As Rick Santorum pointed out on page 4 of his book, *It Takes a Family,* the "...all-too-common caricature of conservatives and their social policies by the liberal elite can be attributed to liberals' fundamentally different vision for America..." (Santorum, 2006).

Indeed, amongst the liberal elite, conservative beliefs were (and are) something to mock. The mockery of men and of conservative Christians in general seemed quite rooted in the feminist movement, which mistakenly ignored the truth: Men and respect *can* go together.

Now, we're not talking about respecting men who abuse. We're talking about healthy respect that both women and men need. Men chauvinists do exist. But a lot of nice guys get the unfair treatment because of erring feminists. Women also have been hampered by feminism: Women do not have to be a smaller version of a man and let a village rear her children. Women can be happy wives and mothers, if that is whom God has called them to be.

Understandably, extreme feminism became a threat to relationship health: As women dove into the mirk and mire of attempting to be "just one of the guys", they forgot that they, as women, are to be prized and protected with great love as found only when Christ lives in the heart of men. It is as though they traded their crowns as co-heirs with

Christ in order to follow a muddy mirage-filled world. Truly, feminism is bad for both male *and* female hearts.

True Freedom for Women

Women can be women without feeling oppressed or depressed because, quite frankly and contrary to the feminist message, being a feminine woman of strength is truly satisfying and beautiful when rooted in Christ. Extreme feminism, rooted in the erroneous social Darwinistic theory of yesteryear, truly cuts at women's hearts and tears apart the family and marriage in the process. Children, who grow up to form the next generation of parents, are hampered and harmed in their development.

The results of an extreme feminism-saturated society prove this point: Dr. Tim Clinton and Dr. George Ohlschalger shared at the very beginning of their book (on page 2) about how women do need love and care of a husband and loving father to their children: "The deterioration of fatherhood in America –by 72.2% of the U.S. population—is considered by some our most serious social ill. Encumbering the development of youth, fatherlessness promotes mental disorders, crime, suicide, poverty, teenaged pregnancy, drug and alcohol abuse, and incarceration." (Clinton & Ohlschlager, 2002) Such startling statistics and tragedies only promote the Biblical definition and aspirations of marriage and family.

First of all, to help fellow young women, let's get this straight: Christian women can be feminine, Godly, and satisfied without believing that they've been suppressed. Christian wives must deprogram from the lies that respecting a husband is dangerous to her freedom as a woman and realize it is good for her and her family. We're not talking about unhealthy forms of abusive submissiveness, by the way.

Returning to the Word of God, Christians enjoy a freeing experience that is untainted by the lies espoused by society. In reality, God desires wives to respect husbands and husbands to love their

44

wives in such a way that harmony –beautiful harmony—can exist in the home where nurturing of spouses and children takes place (Wilhoit, 1995). For this to happen, the "respect" question must be answered. This question can only be answered by Scripture. Countless articles capture the fact that, while feminism attempted to "free" women, it backfired and harmed the family (Kersten, 1994).

To counteract the myths of certain anti-marriage advice, we must first reframe R-E-S-P-E-C-T. First, we must understand the true definition of Christ-like respect and dismiss the hissing lies of the culture that paints an ugly, false picture about what the Bible says regarding marriage. While reframing respect in a healthy, loving way, women can throw out the lie that all men do not want them to be as equal as they. (Women feel such freedom when they realize that they do not have to be "on the defense" about respecting men. They need to understand that men and respect can go together if done in and for Christ.)

Also, when done in a Biblical way, a wife who respects her husband does not mean she disrespects herself. The refreshing truth of the matter is that they do not have to become doormats or slaves to do so, as feminists would purport. Rather, respecting men in a Christ-like way promotes health for the wife and children. Yet men are not exempt from doing their Biblical part:

Husbands are to cherish their wives and are called to love their wives as Christ loves the church. But, for women to be loved and cherished, pornography and other sexual perversion must first be abolished. Today, unlike any other time in modern world history, there exists a severe breakdown of the family and marriage. On the one hand, men have been taught that women should be treated more like mini-men. On the other hand, women are portrayed as sex objects. Both are false.

In the face of a sexually perverse culture, couples need to become conquerors through Christ and, for this to happen, we all need to prayerfully encourage Christ-like conduct for both women and men: Women, while equal to men, are unique and need to be free to appreciate this fact. This means that women can remove the pressure of performing to impress others in the workplace *and* on the homefront. They can do whatever God has called them to do without the pressure of being a supermom who does everything yet feels stressed out all of the time. They do not need to obsess about gaining power through being sexy like a Victoria's Secret model. They are to be cherished and beautiful while honoring Christ. Men, meanwhile, need to grow up into the roles of loving protectors instead of defectors. Consider the modern-day fad of the "man cave", which is usually a room located in a basement where men retreat to play video games, watch sports, etc. It isolates men from their families. While privacy is necessary, family time is essential.

While women need to toss aside the extreme feminism lies, men need to emerge from the "man cave" of entertainment and instead get busy with entrainment of the family and true loving of their wives. When the man feels respected enough to lead and the woman feels loved enough to live without fear, the family unit stabilizes and flourishes –including, of course, the marriage thereof. Indeed, there remains hope for the Christian couple who desires to discard the lies of feminism and return to the beauty of a Christ-centered family life. The Lord remains the same and He desires everyone to come to Him in repentance and acceptance of His Son. Hope in Christ makes all the difference and this hope is expressed in prayer.

Making Prayer a Priority

To further conquer the lies of feminism and liberalism in America, couples and families need to make prayer a priority. Prayer remains an essential ingredient to any marriage. In fact, even a secular publication admitted that "social connectedness and humor were found to be related positively to prayer frequency and more effective coping behaviors." (Spilka & Ladd, 2012) This presents a bedrock for Christian couples: To reject the lies of the world about men and women, couples must pray and focus on Scripture together every day.

When women follow the Scripture about respecting men, they do not disrespect themselves. Instead, out of respect for God, they can respect husbands in a healthy way. For people to end the "Crazy Cycle" portrayed by *Love and Respect* (Eggerichs, 2004), women and men must sacrifice pride on the altar and, ideally, at the marriage altar. When respect and love continue to be implemented, marriages become stronger and both spouses grow in Christ. Over all things, couples must apply Colossians 3:14 (NASB): "Beyond all these things *put on* love, which is the perfect bond of unity."

How to Heal Families and Marriages

As Christians, we believe that happy homes are possible. After the lies of feminism are conquered, love reigns in the family and, as gentle leader of the home, the husband needs to set the trend. Husbands and fathers need respect in order to set the example of how to love. In order for men to not give up, women must give them healthy respect even as the husbands give them love. Respect affords the man dignity and allows him to stop putting up so many barriers in defense of verbal and behavioral disrespect. This grants him the ability to let Christ's love flow uninhibitedly through him to the family: He must love his wife as Christ loves the church. Therefore, the end results are beautiful: The wife encourages the husband's example of Christ-like love by showing him respect, the children are not promoted to anger because of the love factor, and wives feel protected and cherished –free to be the women God desires them to be. The opportunity for families to heal remains ever real because "Jesus Christ *is* the same yesterday and today and forever" (Hebrews 13:8, NASB).

But Some Americans Appear to Hate God and Family...

Flashback to the 2012 Democratic National Convention: A tremendously disturbing event took place. A large number of delegates booed God. It was caught on camera: They booed God three times! The DNC openly exhibited anti-Semitism, anti-God sentiments when they first voted to exclude Israel and God from their platform in reflection of President Obama's policies. Yes, they added them again . . . but only after finding that the public didn't like it. Wait a second! There should never have been a doubt but to include Israel and God! *(Just for the record, we believe it's time to stop anti-Semitism and ask God to bless Israel.)* Then, even as the DNC initially erased Israel and God from their platform, they had the audacity to call other politicians Nazi's.

This is not what our Founders wanted. (And that's putting it mildly.)

Gradually yet stealthily our government grows and our freedoms shrink. A callous forms. People accept the unacceptable until the unimaginable cuts them to the core. As young women, we hope you'll join us in this: It's time to get back to loving God, loving each other, and returning to America's values...including religious liberty! This means spiritual war. Good vs. evil. Religious freedom vs. secularism.

Whether you're a Democrat or Republican or Independent or Libertarian or whatever, please know that this section will help us to learn and never fall ploy to cheap tactics such as those of Adolf Hitler and his government-issued Hitler Youth. Quite frankly, our country exhibits symptoms of societal decay to such an extent that we feel we must include this section as preparation for swift action.

Just how bad is it?

May 2013 shed light on multiple serious cases that target religious freedom. For example, the government has used intimidation tactics to unjustly target Christian and conservative groups because they represent beliefs contrary to the Obama administration. James Dobson, Billy Graham, Franklin Graham, and various other Christian leaders have been heavily targeted by the IRS. Many join Congressman Kevin Brady (R) in asking, "Is this still America?"

But that's not all... Religious freedom for Judeo-Christian members of the military is being threatened, too. The Pentagon released a statement confirming that soldiers could be prosecuted for promoting their faith: "Religious proselytization is not permitted within the Department of Defense...Court martials and non-judicial punishments are decided on a case-by-case basis...". Yes, you read that correctly: The Pentagon is considering prosecuting servicemen and women for sharing their Christian faith. That's stripping away freedom from the very heroes who are fighting to keep and protect it!

As Lt. Gen. William Boykin has said, "If chaplains and other personnel are censored from offering the full solace of the Gospel, there is no religious freedom in the military." We had the honor of meeting Lt. Gen. Boykin and we agree with his stand for freedom.

The Pentagon has confirmed that soldiers could be prosecuted for sharing their Christian faith. Consider the astute response from Tony Perkins, president of the Family Research Council: "Why would military leadership be meeting with one of the most rabid atheists in America to discuss religious freedom in the military? That's like consulting with China on how to improve human rights."

Another vocal beacon, Dr. Ben Carson, spoke truth which applies to our country's politically correct yet anti-Christian freedom situation: "The PC police are out in force at all times. We've reached a point where people are afraid to actually talk about what they want to say, because somebody might be offended. We've got to get over this sensitivity; it keeps people from saying what they really believe. It muffles people, it puts a muzzle on them; and, at the same time, keeps people from discussing important issues while the fabric of their society is being changed."

To further this point, let's ask a different question: What if an NBA star, instead of "coming out", suddenly announced that he was a devout Christian? The secular media would likely turn so silent that the crickets could be heard. Then there would come the vile jokes, snide headlines, etc. Indeed, there exists a strange bias... Startling, isn't it? Now, let's learn more...

CHAPTER EIGHT

Learn from the Past to Win in the Future

"It does not require a majority to prevail, but rather an irate, tireless minority keen to set brush fires in people's minds."- **Samuel Adams**

The government removed religion from curricula and school life. Young people became the most important people group. Rebellion against parents was encouraged. Public education became filled with false information and self-esteem became the goal. Social Darwinism programmed children to believe lies including beliefs that people could act like animals, women were less evolved and inferior to men and needed to "catch up", certain races were genetically inferior, and people with disabilities were less desirable.

Certain groups of people –especially those of Jewish and Christian faiths- became objects of ridicule and hatred. True Christians, who desired simply to practice their faith, encountered obstacle after obstacle as secular beliefs became louder and louder. A leader enraptured the youth's attention as he made them feel "special and superior" to the failed generations of the past.

Sound like America? Well, that's Germany circa 1930.

Now, try to guess this country: A leader became exalted as the only hope for change and progress. Swiftly, government programs began to take over everyday life. People lost ambition and traded it for sexually immoral passions. Sexually explicit images, violence, homosexual propaganda, "me-centered" philosophies, neglect of educational and vocational excellence, and overall disregard for the importance of all life slowly seeped in and flooded out the value of families. "Anything goes" and other liberal agendas reigned in the minds of the majority of entranced citizens. Apathy prevailed and derailed morality.

The USA? Nope. It was Rome (circa 476 A.D.).

Now, take the two preceding descriptions and put them together. What do you have? America today. Such a description of Rome and Germany jolts us awake more than espressos on an empty stomach.

Prior to finishing with a list of action points, we must learn from the past to discern the present and fight for the future with faith in God –not fear of man.

Learn from the Past to Discern the Present and Fight for the Future!

It began in the capitol: Munich. In 1923, an organization young people organized and numbered about 1,000 – a small number compared to Germany's population. By 1940, the group swelled to 8 million. How did this country descend into a society run by a sadistic cause? Here's how the stage was set:

1. **Nazis first appeared harmless as they desired to "improve" Germany.** After WWI, Germany felt ashamed from being defeated by other countries and desired to rise again. The people, vulnerable after having suffered defeat, latched onto the idea of change and new successes for Germany and citizens.

2. **They began subtly and with a smile: Hitler hid the extent of his evil plan and, like a constant drip on sandstone, wore away at the moral foundation of the nation in the guise of progressive change.** (Countless Germans likened it

to such an effect. A little and then a little more and a little more until the nation became so calloused and brainwashed by the repetition of false doctrine.) A spark caught fire and destroyed a forest. The disabled were depicted as a "burden". Dorothea Buck, who grew up in Germany, described the effects of the propaganda: "They depicted the disabled as some sort of burden . . ." The propaganda seemed to promote the idea that the disabled, while given care by the government, were less important to society. (In America, 90% of Down syndrome babies are selectively killed in the womb. We'll cover more about that later.)

3. **They esteemed the power of self-esteem instead of following God's Word.** Giving both self-esteem and lots of presents blinded children and their parents to the stripping of freedoms. A humanistic, liberal agenda laid the groundwork for the construction of idolizing a leader other than God. At one school, boys received a dagger with a message, "Be more than you seem."

4. **They programmed youth at an early age and excluded parents in education all while oppressing women.** Music with corrupted lyrics filled and programmed the minds of young people. One song sung by girls by the League of German Girls called the Bund Deutscher Mädel (BdM) included the lyrics, "The earth creates what is new, the earth takes away what is old. Holy German earth under your health . . ." The children were told they were part of the **new age**. One former school girl said in a documentary, "I thought it was a terrible fate to be a girl." Sports filled children's time so much that they had little time to think and interact with parents. Schools later filtered history with terribly racist, anti-Jewish material. They also excluded true Christian beliefs and replaced them with socialistic, sadistic content. They encouraged youthful rebellion and aggression as "normal".

5. **They excluded God in public life, hosted secular holidays**

scheduled to compete with Christian holy days, and tried to offer an alternative god: In 1939, when Germany invaded Poland, the Schutzstaffel (SS) killed all clergy as well as aristocracy and intelligence. The government removed religion from curricula and school life. When the occasion required it, an allusion to a higher power was utilized but only to propel further cult-like dependence on the leader. By 1942, only 1 in 4 school children believed in God. The tide of setting new ideals in the guise of progress included the devaluing of people groups – including those with perceived imperfections or disabilities.

6. **They appealed to people's weaknesses: Horrific doctrines appealed to the sinful nature of man: a desire for god-like power and satiation of immoral appetites.** Selective "breeding" promoted sex outside of marriage and encouraged unwed mothers who had the right genetics. Had they possessed today's technology, no doubt exists that they would have utilized selective abortions to eliminate perceived imperfections. The government provided medical care and a variation of welfare for the unwed mothers who would produce perceived "perfect" children. Sexual immorality increased. The government orchestrated ways for birth control and "free" sex. The government fertility program, Lebensborn (old German for "Fountain of Life"), attempted to control births. Also, the military encouraged sexual slavery by taking women from concentration camps and enslaving them in a sadistic fashion.

Think of the timeline: German veterans from WWI felt cheated – not defeated. Veterans came home to millions of citizens going hungry and thousands dying of influenza and tuberculosis. Politics polarized with conservatives and socialists each becoming radical under post-war pressure. In the spring of 1918, the extreme left-wing –with most leaders being communist-sympathizing Jewish men—started to cause unrest. The extreme right-wing troops unleashed gunfire on the streets to quell the Communist rebellion. And, slowly but surely, Germans blamed Jewish people for their problems. Inflation soared! Economic chaos and rebellious riots created a climate for a strong leader to take advantage of the needy masses. By 1921, Hitler became the leader of the German Workers Party – later renamed.

By 1924, the German economy bounced back substantially – albeit Germany borrowed from the USA to then pay the post-WWI reparations to the French and British. This false sense of renewed financial security ushered in a time of entertainment and frivolity. But, also in the 1920's, sewage began seeping into the lives of German youth. A cultural movement to return to simple, more natural living and activities arrived. Boys joined camps run by Nazis and loved spending time learning about the great outdoors.

In 1928, the Nazis received only 2.6% of the vote. This meant that 97.4% of the voters rejected the Nazis. But then 1931 brought another financial disaster: Five banks crashed. Approximately 5.5 million Germans became unemployed. More than 20,000 German businesses folded.

Nazis promoted the same message, yet more Germans' situations had changed so terribly that they fell prey to the simple, powerful orations and concepts of Adolf Hitler. Hitler campaigned especially well as he invoked and provoked the instincts of the youth, won parents by their children (e.g. giving swastika painted balloons to little kids).

A tremendous campaigner, Hitler utilized his passionate speaking ability and campaigned in twenty cities in two days by taking advantage of air travel. He pushed his message until calluses formed and the new morals seemed the norm to the people. By 1940, the indoctrination of the nation reached a climax. And millions perished.

The Current Status of America's Society

The excessive emphasis on self-esteem instead of morals, disrespect for adults, indoctrination of "politically correct" (but incorrect) curricula, exclusion of God in the public sphere, and degradation of parents and authorities' importance creates a climate more conducive to a dictator-like disaster. At the time of this writing, our hearts pray that such a thing never occurs in our beloved country. However, we must take note of the current conditions for America's kids:

Christian religious freedom is non-existent in government schools. Students and teachers get into trouble if they dare pray or mention God. Sadly, this situation is not expected to improve any time soon: One of the latest government power grabs is called the Common Core. It ensures that the states build expensive high-tech systems that will track student performance and other personal data and provide that information to the federal government.

To put it simply, the Common Core State Standards Initiative (CCSSI) is a set of national K-12 standards developed primarily by a non-profit: Achieve, Inc. in Washington, D.C exists through the patronage of the National Governors Association (NGA) and the Council of Chief State School Officers (CCSSO). *Most disturbingly, the Common Core was developed without state legislative authority.*

It's unconstitutional, and states have been lured into accepting the Common Core with Race to the Top grant funds and waivers. The federal government is the "enforcer". It is driving states into the "one-size-fits-all" Common Core *regardless of the fact that three federal laws forbid the federal government from directing state educational curriculum.* In addition, the U.S. Constitution and state constitutions uphold the fact that education is a power reserved to the states and their citizens. Yet the Common Core cannot be changed by state legislatives or state school boards. (At the time of this writing, President Obama is pushing this agenda forward and so far only Nebraska, Texas, and Alaska have rejected it.)

And it's not cheap: It is projected that full implementation of the Common Core will cost $16 billion-plus nationwide. **Despite the $4.35 billion Race to the Top grants, about ninety percent of it will be paid for by states and local districts.**

Educators have described the Common Core as being like No

Child Left Behind on steroids! We are very proud of the fact that our family has had a substantial number of teachers for generations. And we are well aware of the classroom reality versus the false ideality of big government socialistic programs. With that said, we are deeply saddened that teachers today are being forced to comply with yet more government regulations. With the Common Core, even more rules will be put into place. Clearly, the Common Core will not only make students suffer, but also hard-working, good teachers. Caring teachers cannot do their job effectively with "big brother" government looking over their shoulders.

Here's what Phyllis Schlafly says about it: "Common Core means federal control of school curriculum, i.e., control by Obama administration left-wing bureaucrats. Federal control will replace all curriculum decisions by state and local school boards, state legislatures, parents and even Congress because Obama bypassed Congress by using $4 billion of Stimulus money to promote Common Core."

With the Common Core on the horizon, we hope that you consider education alternatives. For example, when possible, homeschool. We're not the only ones saying that. Family experts such as James Dobson, Charles Stanley, R.C. Sproul Jr., Erwin Lutzer, the late Dr. D. James Kennedy, and many others have strongly encouraged parents to homeschool their children.

Former military officer and 9/11 Pentagon survivor Brent Hoffman says, "When you consider that homeschool parents spend an average of $500 to $600 a year on each student in comparison to $9,000 to $10,000 for each government school student in the United States, the academic results are astounding. Essentially, homeschool parents are paying less to educate their own children than they spend to educate someone else's children in the government school system. That is a sad commentary on the state of America's public school system. Exceptional teachers are burdened with bureaucracy, standardization and inefficiency. Children in government-run schools spend more time on transportation, recess, lunch, assembly and other activities than reading and math. Parents are seldom involved and genuine leadership is almost non-existent."

Every single day in government schools (a.k.a. public schools), children are indoctrinated with atheism, homosexuality, etc. Most adults would struggle to handle the situations forced on innocent kids in a regular school day. How can we realistically expect little children to successfully deal with such heavy issues and situations?

For the sake of your child, we urge you to consider homeschooling. There are many options and resources available to homeschool. (Learn more about homeschooling at www.hslda.org.) If homeschooling is not an option for you, utilize a private school or supplement your child's education by being involved with their homework and education as a whole. The main thing is to do something to counteract the indoctrination found in government schools; your children need your support!

Today, kids seem to be drugged by pop culture. They seem indoctrinated to form their own world around their own sources of pleasure. But we cannot blame them. Schools, media, and products of all kinds perpetuate the popular mindsets of today's young people. In fact, our current culture seems bent on shaping our country's kids into promiscuous adults before parents realize it! For instance, on Facebook, we felt saddened and shocked: A child of about twelve years old tried to get attention with her pictures only to have adult comments made *by her peers*.

By God's grace, Carrie and I experienced a unique upbringing that included various ingredients to help us learn more. We certainly have much more to learn, but we simply thank God for learning a lot about loving God and people thanks to our parents' commitment to home educate us.

How did America turn the wrong direction? The essence of our research led us to this conclusion: The less our country honors God, the more our country hurts herself. The "anything goes" philosophy is going anywhere *but* the right way. Instead, let's go to God. (That's what the Greatest Generation did, by the way. We've expounded on that in another chapter.)

Rewind to Learn and Fast Forward to Succeed:

If we reverse the mistakes, we see the strengths. Consider each counterpoint to the preceding.

- **With prayerful boldness, expose the harm purported to be "moving forward".** Return to the core, winning values of faith, family, and freedom. **Check the fruits –not the fanfare. "Therefore, you will fully know them by their fruits." That's what Jesus said.** As Jesus warned us in Matthew 7 about people who pretend to be Christians, we must be wary and check the fruits (what people are producing in their lives) of individuals and leaders. As Milton Friedman said, "One of the great mistakes is to judge policies and programs by their intentions rather than their results."
- **Review the Ten Commandments and ask God to give you His view on conduct.** You and I must seek Him first –and not "me first."
- **Educate kids about America *and* the voting process.** If using the e-book, click here to get a DVD for kids called *Learn Our History* by Mike Huckabee. It's about being proud of America's past and how we must vote in the present. And go deeper: Prayerfully consider ways for your children to attend a Christian school or to be home educated by parents or grandparents. Distance education is another option. We cannot believe the lie that children can go to public school and return home without liberal invasion of their minds.
- **Include God in public life. Be bold. Be strong. For the Lord is with you.**
- **Every person counts! And so do votes. Encourage and appeal to people's strengths while helping them register**

to vote. (If using the e-book, click here to learn how to register.) Quiet people can help with behind-the-scenes preparation for conservative events and invite people left and right. (Pun intended.) Serve in any way you can –be it by voicing in speeches, TV interviews, etc. or helping people register to vote or taking people to the polls.

- **LOVE. Yes, we saved the best for last. We must not espouse hate. We must hate evil yet love people.** Jesus said, "A new commandment I give to you, that you love one another: just as I have loved you, you also are to love one another. By this all people will know that you are my disciples, if you have love for one another" (John 13:34-35, ESV)." Love God first and most. And love fellow human beings as yourself. No name-calling. Point out bad behaviors and policies. Hate the policies—not the people. We ban name-calling, but plan on plenty of calling on the Name (of Jesus).

CHAPTER NINE

*3 Common Sense Christian Steps
for America to Soar Again*

"My heart aches for America and its deceived people.
The wonderful news is that our Lord is a God of mercy,
and He responds to repentance." – **Billy Graham**

Star Parker said it well: "You know, we can reason every excuse in the Bible. But a life is a life. All it takes is one acceptance to start allowing all acceptances. The slippery slope to deceit starts with just one falsehood." **You see, moral compromise never pays. Whether it is accepting a vulgar, perverted joke or just shrugging off a slur because "it's just the way it is today", moral compromises never pay.**

While people raise their voices on talk shows that never end, we see many who never bend...their knees. **America, it's time to bow down to stand up.** It's time to put action to our reactions of concern, positive patriotism, and love for fellow man. It's time to rise up with God as our guide! With Him, we can see our country soar again.

C'mon Conservatives! It's time to get our act together:

Unfortunately, even people claiming to be Christians have left Christ out of their politics...even in conservative organizations. We must honor our Creator and remember He created us and we didn't create ourselves. As Billy Graham aptly said, "Our society strives to avoid any possibility of offending anyone –except God."

Conservatives, we must stop flailing our hands at others and begin folding them again. We must seek God before public action. It's time for us to stop copying what we hate! God is not entertained by our prioritization of compromised entertainment. Dirty movies, vulgar talk radio, magazines, and negative messages on social media continue to spurt out the poison. Such entertainment sedates souls. Eventually, people become lulled into a compromised consciousness.

For our country to be alive, we ourselves must be revived. If we continue to allow the liberals to influence our kids and our very own souls through dirty entertainment, we will fall. **And, to win in life and in elections, we cannot claim Christ and entertain ourselves with evil.**

First of all, let us say that we do not claim to be perfect. But we do know the perfect One: Jesus Christ. He gives us such love! We must clean up our lives out of love for Him –not legalism. With that said, let's push the pause button and pray about what we need to give up in order to grasp better things: The movies we watch, the games we play, the Facebook stuff we post (and view), the language we enjoy, the pictures we hang –all of these either enhance or fog our vision. In order to win, we must detox from sin. Take a break from bad forms of entertainment and instead devote the time to only things that build your faith and family.

In the course of human events, a callousness of conscience can occur and numb people of great beliefs and huge potential from accomplishing what's right. People never see it coming. It's gradual. It's subtle. And it's fatal. But there's hope as we seek the Lord's best and turn to Him. There is still time – but precious little. Take the advice of our Founding Fathers. Read their words of wisdom:

"Only a virtuous people are capable of freedom. As nations become corrupt and vicious, they have more need of masters."
–Benjamin Franklin

"Neither the wisest constitution nor the wisest laws will secure the liberty and happiness of a people whose manners are universally corrupt."
–Samuel Adams

"It is certainly true that a popular government cannot flourish without virtue in the people."
–Richard Henry Lee

"To the kindly influence of Christianity we owe that degree of civil freedom, and political and social happiness which mankind now enjoys . . . Whenever the pillars of Christianity shall be overthrown, our present republican forms of government, and all blessings which flow from them, must fall with them."
–Jedediah Morse

"While just government protects all in their religious rights, true religion affords to government its surest support."
–George Washington

Such quotes present a vivid contrast to today's popular language. In our current culture in particular, common sense continues to plummet to uncommon lows. Consider a story demonstrative of this:

Recently, a classroom full of teachers looked at their instructor. She cracked a coy smile and shook her head. Looking up and then looking down at the class, she said something like this: "The conservatives of the Far Right would like to take us back to a place where creativity is coldly repressed. They want to take us to a style of poor education for America's children."

When we heard about this, Carrie and I thought, "But how can it get any worse for our generation?" Every single day, kids in public schools are subjected to anti-God curricula and sexual perversion portrayed as "normal". For example, public education and the media exalt homosexuality and attack anyone who opposes it.

Kids today need to understand why marriage is between one man and one woman. God designed it that way; that is what it will always be. It cannot be redefined. Marriage cannot be anything else but between one man and one woman. Sadly, today's children are being taught the opposite.

These days it's "controversial" to say that marriage is between one man and one woman –but it's true. God chooses our sex/gender...not humans. He knows what He's doing when He creates each person. That's why it's so disturbing to see how people try to take His place by turning marriage into something He never made it to be... The Lord loves everyone, but He does not approve of homosexual practices. Such behavior is perverse and unnatural. He has the best in mind for each person He creates which is why the Bible clearly warns against homosexuality.

From Genesis on, the Bible praises the marriage of a man and a woman, but it always speaks very critically of homosexual behavior whenever it is mentioned (i.e. 1 Corinthians 6:9-11, Jude 7, Romans 1:18-32, Leviticus 18:22).

Scripture clearly teaches that God designed marriage to be between one man and one woman –it can be nothing else but that. For example, Jesus said in Matthew 19:4-6, "Have you not read that he who created them from the beginning made them male and female, and said, 'Therefore a man shall leave his father and his mother and hold fast to his wife, and the two shall become one flesh'? So they are no longer two but one flesh. What therefore God has joined together, let not man separate."

In 2013, the Pew Research Center released a report showing that media coverage was biased by a factor of 5 to 1 in favor of same-sex "marriage". This is an attack on Judeo-Christian values and it's persecution against marriage. Chuck Colson summarized the situation well when he said, "We're not going to have any society left if we don't protect the marriage bond. And the homosexual movement is trying to unravel it."

It's interesting that the far left likes to claim tolerance (especially towards homosexuality), yet they cannot tolerate our conservative Christian values. **Today, just as Nazi Germany prior to WWII stealthily, slyly blamed Jews for the nation's problems, so are Christians blamed in our nation today.** People blame "Christians" for slavery and oppression of women. Yet they ignore the fact that the true Christians led movements to provide better treatment for all!

As President Ronald Reagan rightly said, "Without God, there is no virtue, because there's no prompting of the conscience. Without God, we're mired in the material, that flat world that tells us only what the senses perceive. Without God, there is a coarsening of the society. And without God, democracy will not and cannot long endure. If we ever forget that we're one nation under God, then we will be a nation gone under."

When we choose compromised values and disinvite God, we invite all kinds of evil. Yet there is hope! If enough people pray and obey today, God could revive America to soar higher than ever.

Modern America is at war: a cultural, spiritual war of good against evil. Clearly, good and evil exist. It's not politically correct to say it, but it's true. We "... are not wrestling with flesh and blood [contending only with physical opponents], but against the despotisms, against the powers, against [the master spirits who are] the world rulers of this present darkness, against the spirit forces of wickedness in the heavenly (supernatural) sphere."[6]

It's hard to believe how far our country regresses in the name of "progress". People with extremely liberal beliefs desire to "correct" our country and put her in her place as a mere peer to other countries

6   Eph. 6:12

abroad. But, to be frank, our country needs to be an example –not a sample of Europe!

Reality and extreme liberal thought do not match. The fact of the matter is that our country was founded by Christians who desired people to have a choice to worship as they pleased and not oppressed by a government-run church. True Christians desire to honor God but realize it's up to Him to work in the hearts of people to turn to Him.

Humans cannot make other humans Christians. Consider the summary given by Liberty University's Vice-President, Dr. Elmer Towns:

"[T]here are still many evidences of Christian influence in America's laws, business, practice, and the average way of American life. The Christian influences in American culture today are largely the remnants of an earlier time when biblical Christianity was a dominant influence on the formative culture of a young nation.

"Throughout history, when revivals came to a region or country, their culture was influenced by Christian principles. When a nation is Christianized, it doesn't mean that everyone has become a Christian or that Christianity controls every citizen. It simply means the Christian principles and virtues have become a big influence upon that country's culture" (Towns, 2007).

Today, America needs to remember that prayer can –and should!—be encouraged and not discouraged. In yesteryears, there exist myriad examples of how this can be done. For instance, we'd be wise to heed a national proclamation of prayer in 1812, as made by President James Madison. Please read the proclamation, heed its intention, and share the inspiration:

Proclamation.

WHEREAS *the Congress of the United States, by a joint resolution of the two Houses, have signified a request, that a day may be recommended, to be observed by the People of the United States, with religious solemnity, as a day of public Humiliation, and Prayer; and whereas such a recommendation will enable the several religious denominations and societies so disposed, to offer, at one and the same time, their common vows and adorations to Almighty God, on the solemn occasion produced by the war, in which he has been pleased to permit the injustice of a foreign power to involve these United States;*

I do therefore recommend the third Thursday in August next, as a convenient day to be set apart for the devout purposes of rendering to the Sovereign of the Universe and the Benefactor of mankind, the public homage due to his holy attributes; of acknowledging the transgressions which might justly provoke the manifestations of His divine displeasures; of seeking His merciful forgiveness, His assistance in the great duties of repentance and amendment; and especially of offering fervent supplications, that in the present season of calamity and war, He would take the American People under his peculiar care and protection; that he would guide their public councils, animate their patriotism, and bestow His blessing on their arms; that He would inspire all nations with a love of justice and of concord, and with a reverence for the unerring precept of our holy religion, to do to others as they would require others to do to them; and finally, that, turning the hearts of our enemies from the violence and injustice which sway their councils against us, He would hasten a restoration of the blessings of Peace.

Given at Washington the 9th day of July, in the year of our Lord one thousand eight hundred and twelve.

James Madison.

By the President.

James Monroe,
Secretary of State

So what was your reaction to the preceding? Disbelief? Relief? For us, such historical documents leap out of the background and into the foreground as examples that we, as conservative Christians, have proof and can negate the arguments of anti-Christians.

With all things considered, isn't it utterly preposterous that certain liberal leaders leave out "under God" in the Pledge of Allegiance and "endowed by their Creator" in the Declaration of Independence? You see, even in the Declaration of Independence, our Founding Fathers declared dependence on God, our Creator. We need God, and that reminds us to share a personal story:

Stacie and Carrie with Senator Rick Santorum

After Rick Santorum keynoted and with a Fox News microphone still positioned at the podium, I (Stacie) rose from my seat and approached the podium. I spoke from my heart before offering a closing prayer. I shared this:

We cannot invoke God's blessing on our nation as we constantly provoke Him by killing His creation and disinviting Him from our nation. We must repent. We as a nation must repent of national sins such as allowing and funding the murder of over 55 million babies.

And we must repent personally. We cannot clean up our country if our own hands remain dirty. Come to the Lord with a humble heart. Let's confess our sins to Him. We Americans cannot stand up and fight without first taking time to bow down. Utilize the pre-prayer strategy. Fold hands, repent individually, and then proceed with God's power for this emergency hour so that America will not crash.

Here's an illustration: An eagle cannot fly without having sat with folded wings and then unfolding them into a burst of triumphant flight. So we must fold our hands and then unfold them in God-honoring action. We must bow down in repentance as we seek God first. Otherwise, our efforts will be in vain. This battle cannot be fought by a political party, a leader, or money. **This battle can only be won with God.**

In order to expect, look for, and hope in Him, we must turn from sin and look up to His Son. When we turn from our own sins, we welcome Him in and His power is at work in us. We know this from experience. We've prayed at the bedside of Christian patriots. Never, ever did they regret doing things God's way. When we look to Him, we're radiant and our faces are never ashamed. "Those who look to him are radiant; their faces are never covered with shame" (Ps. 34:5, NIV 1984).

We must look up with confidence in Him and wait for Him while we wait on hand and foot to do the right thing before we see the return of our King! Only then can we fully claim Isaiah 40:31 (AMP):

"But those who wait for the Lord [who expect, look for, and hope in Him] shall change and renew their strength

*and power; they shall lift their wings and mount up [close
to God] as eagles [mount up to the sun]; they shall run
and not be weary, they shall walk and not faint or become
tired."-Is. 40:31 (AMP)*

In conclusion, let's all prayerfully consider the following.

"3 Common Sense Christian Steps for America to Soar Again":

1. **Repent.** First of all, repentance is not a bad word. It's a good word! Repent nationally. (Turn from bad, anti-God ways like killing the unborn.) And, first, let's repent personally. (Review the Ten Commandments, confess, repent, and surrender to the Lord's ways.)

   Last week, we met another woman in physical pain. Yet she refused our offer to pray with her. Instead, she thanked us for sending thoughts. The darkness in her eyes conveyed the worst pain possible. She refused prayer... A common pitfall is reliance on "positive thinking and energy" instead of prayer. That's New Age philosophy, which is an old lie. We must turn only to God –not our own "power". Rely and share His power with others.

   And we cannot coast along while ignoring the fatally injured along life's highway. Sometimes people feel like something's wrong...because they're actually doing what's wrong. It's time for us all to repent and follow Jesus 100%. Amen? Make time and share with the lost. Have "forward faith": Move forward. Share the Good News via actions and words. It's time to repent of complacency and dormancy. (Check out a powerful sermon called "What We Need is Repentance" by Rev. James J. Hudzinski.)

   So repent of silence and share the Good News today! If people reject it, they reject the Lord -not you. Souls are at stake. Don't hesitate. Instead... "Sing to the Lord, all the earth! Tell of his salvation from day to day" (I Chronicles 16:23). And remember that Jesus is coming back and He'll make everything right in the end! Get on God's Side: Let Jesus inside your heart now. Later may not come.

2. **Revere.** Trust in God –not man. And apply Psalm 56:10-11 (ESV): "In God, whose word I praise, in the LORD, WHOSE WORD I PRAISE, in God I trust; I shall not be afraid. What can man do to me?" Recognize God as God. God loves you! Obey Him with love –not legalistic bondage. Doing things His way out of love for Him makes all the difference. But, again, first be sure to receive His gift of eternal life. (Learn more and get prayer at www.PrayingPals.org.)

3. **Persevere.** Persevere with faith and prayer. "With God's help we will do mighty things..." (Psalm 60:12, NLT). **Again, it's time to bow down and stand up. We must stand up for those who can't!** "Speak up for those who cannot speak for themselves; ensure justice for those being crushed" (Proverbs 31:8, NLT).

In closing, let us pray: "Lord God, we thank You that You are always true, loving, gracious, and faithful. We plead Your mercy on America. Please protect and deliver us from evil! We ask for You to guide the hearts of leaders, candidates, and their families into a relationship with You. We confess our sins of focusing on the bad and ask that You would give us Your vision of what's good. We repent and we receive You now as Lord and Redeemer, Jesus. We thank You that no problem is too big for You! We put our trust in You, O God. Please bless America! In Jesus' Name, Amen."

ACTION POINT: Read a U.S. History book that hasn't been pre-programmed by liberals. Enjoy the books by Mike Huckabee and David Barton. Also, Liberty University recommends *A Patriot's Guide to American History* by Larry Schweikart.

CHAPTER TEN

Revival Begins with Each One of Us

"Nothing of eternal consequence happens apart from prayer."
–Charles G. Finney

As John Adams aptly said, "Our Constitution was made only for a moral and religious people. It is wholly inadequate to the government of any other." Clearly, President Adams understood the fact that for freedom to survive, faith in God must be alive. If people no longer fear consequences for their actions, society suffers serious repercussions.

Sin. It's a word strangely absent from most Americans' vocabularies. Yet it is sadly present and rampant. Sin is falling short of God's standards, ignoring Him as God, and doing anything that feels good even if the Bible says it's bad. Everyone sins. But only our perfect Lord saves! He deserves all glory and praise!

Think about it: If people cannot admit that they are sinners, they miss the mark and fail to give the due glory to the Savior. So let us both say it clearly: Only Jesus Christ is perfect. And we are sinners saved by the most loving, righteous, gracious Lord Jesus! "Christ Jesus came into the world to save sinners—of whom I am the worst. But for that very reason I was shown mercy so that in me, the worst of sinners, Christ Jesus might display his unlimited patience as an example for those who would believe on him and receive eternal life" (1 Timothy 1:15-16). Do you know the awesomeness of knowing God personally? Jesus Christ loves you and offers to save you from the terminal effects of sin and hell. Come to Him and let Him make you well! Pray, repent, and receive Him today. (Learn more at the "Know God" page at PrayingPals.org.)

If people do not admit they need the Lord and instead latch onto liberal dogma about "anything goes", they choose a destructive existence and their children suffer a breakdown in knowing right from wrong. Quite frankly, daily headlines reveal only the first rumblings of immorality's dangerous path (i.e. shootings, kidnappings, child-killings, increases in violent crimes of all kinds, etc.) Extreme liberalism is not working, but a campaign to blame Christians continues as a last-ditch effort to save face.

Concurrently and not coincidentally, rumors about Christians run rampant: Liberal professors espouse hatred for Christians on whom they place full blame for problems in society. It's atrocious, but very popular amongst American academia to blame Christians almost entirely for social ills ranging from the horrors of slavery to the oppression of women. (In reality, loving God and neighbor really allows for a productive, equal society in which no people group is deemed sub-human.)

Ravi Zacharias, a world-renowned lecturer and apologist, put it well in his excellent book, *The End of Reason:*

> "Here you have one of their own [atheists] telling us that there are 'superior' humans and 'inferior' ones. We have been down the atheist road before, and it ended in a Holocaust. It was belief in absolute morality, in true God-given egalitarianism, that brought slavery to an end."

Now, there have been people since the time of Jesus who have pretended to be full of faith yet are actually full of hate. And that's why Jesus Christ warned His followers that we must know who's a real Christian by the fruit of their lives (what they are producing in their lives). Jesus said, "Yes, just as you can identify a tree by its fruit, so you can identify people by their actions" (Matthew 7:20, NLT).

For many churches and non-profit organizations in the red, white, and blue, it's a "Code Blue". They've lost their passion for the lost. They entertain instead of entrain those who are supposed to carry the Lord's love and Gospel to others. (But there are still Biblically-based, thriving ministries and churches in America. The secular press do not tend to feature them. But they still exist, and that's encouraging.)

Yet too many of America's churches seek to please the world rather than Christ. Dr. D. James Kennedy said it well:

> "We've probably all heard the cliché 'the church is full of hypocrites'. Why do people say that? Because the church is full of hypocrites –that's why they say it. And why is the church full of hypocrites? It's because the church discipline in most churches is as dead as a dodo bird."

Complete hypocrites do not know they're hypocrites because they have yet to know Jesus personally. They have allowed the world to influence them more than the Word. They've traded passion for calculated performance. The result? Americans don't know what it means to be a Christian. They see church more as a time-taking, socializing addition to an already busy schedule. If only they knew what they're missing, or rather *Whom* they're missing...

It's time for revival in the pulpits as well as the pews. It's time for each person –including you and me—to sit down before the Lord and repent. (Yes, we said it: Repent. Like sin, it's not a buzzword. But it should be.)

Consider what Holocaust survivor and Christian rescuer of many Jewish people, Corrie ten Boom, said in her book, *I Stand at the Door and Knock* (p. 45):

"Being made holy is a step toward revival. Somebody asked the evangelist, Gypsy Smith, 'What can I do to achieve revival in my church?' He replied, "Go to your room, take a piece of chalk, draw a circle on the floor, and kneel down in the center of the circle. And then pray, 'Lord, send revival to my church, and may it begin in the center of this circle.'"

"That was a sharp reply, wasn't it, but he was right. It is God's will that we may become holy. The Lord Jesus clearly said that we needed to be born again, that we can be God's children, and that we will then take our sins to the Lord." (ten Boom, 2008)

Yes! Revival begins with each one of us. To revive, repentance remains essential. Repentance and prayer go together. They remain essential to the fabric of our country: **We cannot change America without God's help. And we must care more about what God thinks than what our neighbors think.** Think about it: No person is liked by everyone. So why live like it's possible to be liked by all? Why be politically correct yet eternally incorrect? What's important is to do what God wants us to do...even if people dislike us in the process. Experience and share the love and truth of the Lord! In the end, it will be more than worth it. Oh, to hear Him say, "Well done!" (Let's live out I Corinthians 13 every single day.)

Also, we don't have to try to make the Gospel more "attractive" to unbelievers. The Lord Himself exceeds all our dreams! He attracts. We just need to pray and love like Jesus. And that's a fact.

America needs more preachers who care about saving souls in America instead of saving their popularity. Amen? (We're so thankful that we have wonderful pastors at our church.) And neither can we silently wait for revival apart from praying for it. Consider these words from Charles Finney:

"Churches grow when people pray effectively to get

people saved, receive resources, remove barriers and enrich the service of Christ. There are two kinds of means requisite to promote a revival: the one to influence God, the other to influence men. Prayer is an essential link in the influence that leads to a revival, as much so as truth is. Some have zealously used truth to convert men, and laid very little stress on prayer. They have preached, and talked, and distributed tracts with great zeal, and then wondered that they had so little success. And the reason was that they forgot to use the other branch of the means, effectual prayer. They overlooked the fact that truth, by itself, will never produce the effect, without the Spirit of God, and that the Spirit is given in answer to prayer."

Now, do you join us in desiring to cast aside all that's not of God? Are you ready to be revived by Him? Well, instead of turning this into a theological tome, let us condense it down to **R.E.V.I.V.A.L.**

R: Repent and return to God's Word. Joel 2:12-13 (NLT) proclaims it: "That is why the Lord says, 'Turn to me now, while there is time. Give me your hearts. Come with fasting, weeping, and mourning. Don't tear your clothing in your grief, but tear your hearts instead.' Return to the Lord your God, for he is merciful and compassionate, slow to get angry and filled with unfailing love. He is eager to relent and not punish."

E: End the entertainment syndrome. The entertainment syndrome essentially equates trying to use technology to touch hearts instead of submitting to the Holy Spirit.

Now, using technology is great when it's a tool and not a substitution for true worship. If people try to use technology instead of letting God use them, it's like trying to replace the sun with an LED light. It never works. It gives an artificial sense of doing something. "And so the Lord says, 'These people say they are mine. They honor me with their lips, but their hearts are far from me. And their worship of me is nothing but man-made rules learned by rote'" (Isaiah 29:13, NLT).

V: Value what God values. The Ten Commandments protect; they don't inflict. They show us what is right and wrong. In America and beyond, every moral substitution only creates more problems and not solutions. To review, here's the direct quote from Exodus 20:1-17 (NLT, bold-faced added): *"Then God gave the people all these instructions:*

> *'I am the Lord your God, who rescued you from the land of Egypt, the place of your slavery.* **You must not have any other god but me.**
>
> **'You must not make for yourself an idol of any kind** *or an image of anything in the heavens or on the earth or in the sea. You must not bow down to them or worship them, for I, the Lord your God, am a jealous God who will not tolerate your affection for any other gods. I lay the sins of the parents upon their children; the entire family is affected—even children in the third and fourth generations of those who reject me. But I lavish unfailing love for a thousand generations on those who love me and obey my commands.*
>
> **'You must not misuse the name of the Lord your God.** *The Lord will not let you go unpunished if you misuse his name.*

'Remember to observe the Sabbath day by keeping it holy. You have six days each week for your ordinary work, but the seventh day is a Sabbath day of rest dedicated to the Lord your God. On that day no one in your household may do any work. This includes you, your sons and daughters, your male and female servants, your livestock, and any foreigners living among you. For in six days the Lord made the heavens, the earth, the sea, and everything in them; but on the seventh day he rested. That is why the Lord blessed the Sabbath day and set it apart as holy.*

'Honor your father and mother. Then you will live a long, full life in the land the Lord your God is giving you.*

'You must not murder.

'You must not commit adultery.

'You must not steal.

'You must not testify falsely against your neighbor.

'You must not covet your neighbor's house. You must not covet your neighbor's wife, male or female servant, ox or donkey, or anything else that belongs to your neighbor.'"*

I: Invest in outreach. With inner transformation comes outer evangelization. Once we know and live in fellowship with God, His love overflows! Evangelism can't help but happen. And more people unite and do what's right as they experience the bliss of loving God and each other together. Copy and paste this example from Paul: "We loved you so much that we shared with you not only God's Good News but our own lives, too" (1 Thessalonians 2:8).

V: View things from God's perspective...not man's. It's dangerous when people forget God's Word and try to do things as led by the devil's competition-driven methods. Consider Christ's words in Mark 8:33 (NLT): "Jesus turned around and looked at his disciples, then reprimanded Peter. 'Get away from me, Satan!' he said. 'You are seeing things merely from a human point of view, not from God's.'"

A: Apply God's Word fully...not half-heartedly. When people apply Scripture in context and implement expository preaching into services, great results occur because God is given His rightful place: the highest. "All Scripture is inspired by God and is useful to teach us what is true and to make us realize what is wrong in our lives. It corrects us when we are wrong and teaches us to do what is right. God uses it to prepare and equip his people to do every good work" (II Timothy 3:16-17, NLT).

L: Love God and neighbor as He commands...even when others don't understand. This will happen often. But it doesn't matter when you realize it's the Lord Jesus you serve. And knowing the Lord exceeds any reward. We will see Him make all things right in the end! Until then, let's heed the words in Mark 12:29-31 (NLT): "Jesus replied, 'The most important commandment is this: "Listen, O Israel! The Lord our God is the one and only Lord. And you must love the Lord your God with all your heart, all your soul, all your mind, and all your strength." The second is equally important: "Love your neighbor as yourself." No other commandment is greater than these.'"

In summary, we must seek the Reviver and not obsess over revival. To close this chapter, let's pray together:

> "Lord God, we acknowledge You made us. You alone are God and deserve our worship. We confess our country's national sins of ignoring You yet pleading Your protection. We confess we entertain ourselves and ignore what You want us to do. We confess we've attempted to do what only You can do and we've failed miserably at it. Forgive us, Lord. Have mercy on our land, we pray. We ask for Your Holy Spirit to send revival and awakening throughout our land...We pray that hearts of leaders would be softened in Your Hand, Lord. We pray that minds would be purified and that You would be glorified. We pray that we all would know You and that people would welcome Your loving, beloved Son, Jesus, instead of using His Name in a profane way. We pray for this, Lord. We pray this for others and for ourselves. We fall at Your feet and ask Your mercy. And we lift up our veterans and ask You to help them in ways our government has failed them. Help us to help others. We thank You. We trust in You... In You, dear God, we trust. In Jesus' Name, Amen."

ACTION POINT: Pray and read His Word before you get up and let it be the last thing you read before you go to sleep. With God's help, we can live it. Praise God that He responds when we repent and receive His Son. Hallelujah! There exists endless hope in the Lord. Never give up praying for our country. He can and will answer in the best way!

PART III

*Americans: How to Take Positive
Actions of Faith in Negative Times*

CHAPTER ELEVEN

How to Abort Abortion

...*because "Thou Shalt Not Kill" Includes Unborn Babies*

"I praise you, for I am fearfully and wonderfully made. Wonderful are your works; my soul knows it very well." – **Psalm 139:14 (ESV)**

Special Needs = Special Purpose

Trig Palin is an American with a special purpose! People with perceived disabilities enable us to see glimmers of God's love. We see that in Trig Palin. For us, the appreciation and love for special needs kids runs deep and long. We have always believed them to be God's gifts –not defects. But not everyone feels this way, tragically...

Recently, Bill Maher and other celebrities essentially verbally abused and bullied little Trig Palin, who has Down syndrome. So we formed a Facebook fan page for Trig. Within days, thousands upon thousands joined the page as fans of precious Trig. We thanked God for it. We thanked God for it because of various reasons. One was simply to encourage the Palin's, who did the right thing to choose life. And, two, we thank God for the opportunity to show others how important and needed are those with special needs. Here's how we posted it on our fan page for Trig Palin (www.facebook.com/trigpalinisagift):

> "So someone wondered if this page was for monetary exploitation. No way. As Christians who see Trig as a treasure (who is already in the public eye), we feel it's time to give him and his family some encouragement for a change. This page is genuine, grassroots, and very needed in a sick society that allows for abuse mislabeled as "humor". (Bill Maher is not funny. He needs prayers...not laughs.) As a co-founder of this fan page for Trig, I come from a small town where people know how important it is to love people sincerely...and not take a reward for it. Hey, we get no money or reward other than the supreme satisfaction of seeing a little guy (who is already in the public eye) get the love and appreciation he so deserves. Let's overcome evil with good. Let's value the life of every American. Are you with us? If so, please share this Trig Palin page to give the appreciation and love that Trig Palin so deserves! Maybe moms and dads will choose life because of seeing how treasured Trig is... God bless all of you as you treasure one of His gifts: Trig Palin."
>
> -Stacie Ruth (and Carrie Beth), who are just sisters who love God, America, and (of course) Trig Palin

You see, Trig is on the winning side! And that's according to the Lord: "Beware that you do not despise or feel scornful toward or think little of one of these little ones, for I tell you that in heaven their angels always are in the presence of and look upon the face of My Father Who is in heaven" (Matthew 18:10). Tragically, certain laws and leaders reflect an anti-life (particularly lives with special needs) belief system.

At a doctor's office, we heard a physically and mentally challenged boy say, "I love Obama! I love Obama! I love Obama!" Little did he realize that President Obama would have condoned the killing of him in the womb.

Did you realize that most disabled unborn babies are aborted selectively? We cannot ignore this. To ignore it is to silently allow it. Speak up. Pray hard. Reach out.

Ever noticed how you don't see as many sweet kids with Down syndrome? In America, 90% of Down syndrome unborn babies are being aborted - that's genocide of the unborn! You read that correctly: 90% of Down syndrome babies get killed before they can cry. Let babies with Down syndrome live! People with Down syndrome shine as loving treasures.

One such treasure is Robin Hiser. We learned about her through Joni Eareckson Tada's ministry, *Joni and Friends*: Over 50 years ago when Robin was born with Down syndrome, her parents were told that she would be institutionalized. However, her loving family rejected that idea. They took Robin home and brought her up right alongside her siblings. A regular attendee and volunteer at Joni and Friends Family Retreats, she inspires all around her. Robin's passion for Jesus Christ shines as she speaks to her precious Savior with warmth and devotion. If using the e-book, <u>click here</u> to watch a video of Robin's story on the television show *Joni and Friends*.

Robin's life is precious and valuable. People with Down syndrome should be cherished and protected –not aborted! It's time to stop it. With God's help, we can.

Stacie and Carrie singing "In God We Still Trust" at the Gift of Life premiere

85

The subject of protecting the unborn goes further than stopping abortion. One particular event opened our eyes to even more details about this topic: Near Christmas, Governor Mike Huckabee requested that Stacie sing the National Anthem for his pro-life movie premiere event. We also sang our signature song from our latest album, *In God We Still Trust*. Prior to singing, we stayed in the green room. Little did we know what a special treat awaited us there!

Stacie and Carrie with Elisha Lancaster

Eight year old Elisha Lancaster's smile sparkled more than her shiny necklace. Both matched her gorgeous Christmas dress. We visited and laughed so much. It lifted our hearts. Elisha, one of the movie's cast members, was adopted . . . as an embryo. Yes, an embryo. As we hugged the precious child and saw her overjoyed parents, we thought, "This confronts the issue of embryonic stem cell research head-on! Imagine if Elisha had been destroyed for research!"

The experience so near Jesus' birthday reminded us of the miracle of His birth. Of course, it's mind-bogglingly miraculous that God sent His Son. But it's also tremendous how God worked around the government.

The government didn't want the Child to live either. A slaughter of little boys ensued after Jesus' birth. Selectively, King Herod issued an order to kill all boys around Jesus' age. Such weeping and wailing rocked the homes where mothers once rocked their babies. But God provided a way to save Jesus from death so that He could save us by living as an example, dying, and rising again to conquer sin and death. "Now after they had gone, behold, an angel of the Lord appeared to Joseph in a dream and said, Get up! [Tenderly] take unto you the young Child and His mother and flee to Egypt; and remain there till I tell you [otherwise], for Herod intends to search for the Child in order to destroy Him" (Matthew 2:13, AMP).

Today, the United States government issues an order against many babies' lives. How? By funding abortions. Planned Parenthood receives much money from taxpayers. And they don't help people plan parenthood. They plan baby-killing.

Startling statistics reveal a tendency in our country of selective killing: In a recent LifeNews.com article[7], a similar statistic sends shudders: Only about 10% of Down syndrome children get a birthday. Again, 90% are killed in utero. (Other countries are paving the way for abortion acceptance: In China, millions of baby girls get killed in the womb because they're not boys.) Approximately 54 million Americans aren't enjoying America because they were killed while in the womb.

Today, childless parents struggle to find children to adopt in America because so many of such adoptable children have been killed before they could be rocked and treasured. Adoption remains the only option –not abortion. If only more young mothers understood how many wonderful parents yearn for their empty arms to hold a baby...

7   http://www.lifenews.com/2011/10/26/down-syndrome-kid-inspires-with-i-survived-abortion-sign/

A poor Middle Eastern teenager carried her child to term so that He could carry and conquer the burdens of sin and death. Today, results of sin and death include abortion. And Jesus desires us to abort abortion and embrace loving everyone. We believe Jesus desires us to cry out for the babies that never cry. He loves babies. He even came as one.

We encourage all expectant moms to give their babies birthdays. And, whether a woman has had an abortion or not, God loves each woman and offers a fresh start in faith.

Today, throughout America and the world, millions upon millions of babies never breathe. They're killed before they can cry. Today, some people say, "It's a fetus. It's not a person." Well, no "tissue" becomes a person. The fetus is a baby. Yes, a baby is a person. And even embryos deserve to be adopted. (Remember Elisha?)

Yes, it's worth repeating: Jesus loves babies. He alone knows most what babies feel. He came as one. But the devil hates life and, even when Jesus arrived, unleashed a killing spree (approved by the government) to kill the little boys (two years old and younger) in Bethlehem and its districts.

Today, the government promotes a silent slaughter. And we cry out for the babies that never cry. Abort abortion. Life isn't a "choice" to make. Life must be the only option. Abortion –unborn baby killing– hurts the heart of God. He creates each child with tender, loving care. **And He loves each mother-to-be and welcomes every woman who has had an abortion to get a fresh start with new birth in faith.**

Baby Jesus, born to an unwed, impoverished mother, shattered the darkness of a night in a tiny town…and the world. (Let Jesus into the inn of your heart. Go to <u>www.prayingpals.org/knowgod</u>.)

The real choice remains: Will you passively live while preborn babies get killed? Or will you do something lovingly and positively helpful to rescue the children of tomorrow? Please say, "Yes."

ACTION POINT: Many Elisha's need to be born. Become a pro-life pro. Tomorrow's children will thank you.

Get Active to Stop Abortion:

1. Contact Congress and use our helpful contact information at the back of the book.
2. Send letters to editors, bloggers, and all media.
3. Vote, vote, vote! (Yes, it's worth repeating.)
4. Refuse to support products and organizations that fund abortions.
5. Don't buy tickets to concerts by those supporting abortion.

CHAPTER TWELVE

Ways to Win the "Quality of Life" Debate

"... We will stand amazed to see the topside of the
tapestry and how God beautifully embroidered each
circumstance into a pattern for our good and His glory."
— **Joni Eareckson Tada**

We'll never forget it: With heavy hearts, we fell to our knees beside the bedside of a dying friend, "Sue", and prayed. She was starving to death and dying a painful death. Her child-turned-caregiver had stopped her anti-depressant medication and, of course, this cessation caused a depression to descend upon her and made her feel like she wanted to die. Her liberal children felt it was her "right to die". All she needed was a simple anti-depressant. Sue had other treatable health problems but treatment was refused. A "right to die" doctor agreed to have her put on liberal hospice care because of it. Her heart medicines were then withheld and she was not given nourishment for about two weeks.

Our hands were legally tied. But we tried hard. We fed her ice cream. We contacted Bobby Schindler, Terri Schiavo's brother. (But he, too, could not help us in spite of all he has learned and done since his sister's death.)

"Sue" died.

Our culture of life needs CPR or else it will soon entirely morph into a culture of death. We're already in cardiac arrest: Elderly people receive less encouragement to live. Certain doctors, taught by liberal professors who promote a "quality of life" determination, don't help certain people as much as younger, "greater contributors" to society.

Renowned pro-life fighter Fr. Frank Pavone aptly said, "When people ask me about the 'right to die', I respond, 'Don't worry – you won't miss out on it!'"

A right is a moral claim. We do not have a claim on death; rather, death has a claim on us! Some see the "right to die" as parallel to the "right to life." In fact, however, they are opposite. The "right to life" is based on the fact that life is a gift that we do not possess as a piece of property (which we can purchase or sell or give away or destroy at will), but rather is an inviolable right. It cannot be taken away by another or by the person him/herself. The "right to die" is based, rather, on the idea of life as a "thing we possess" and may discard when it no longer meets our satisfaction. The "Right to die" philosophy says there is such a thing as a "life not worth living." For a Christian, however, life is worthy in and of itself, and not because it meets certain criteria that others or we might set."

The quality of life debate circulates a rumor that each person deserves to die with dignity. This is wrong. Each person's life has quality. **God decided to make you, and it's up to Him to decide when to take you.** The entire falsely labeled "compassionate death" is concocted out of a philosophy that people are not worth as much if they're malformed, broken, or elderly. Then, after significant campaigning within the medical community, the false idea of loved ones being "selfish" to keep their relatives alive keeps popping up. (It's not selfish, by the way. It's called lovingly caring for your loved one.)

We sincerely believe and pray that God might use this chapter to change your life or save the lives of others. **It's time to become a pro-life pro.**

First of all, we agree with the National Right to Life and the Alliance Defense Fund. In addition to abortion, another anti-life agenda exists: a person's right to die. Today, a hell-driven attack on human life continues to assail America and other nations.

The elderly, under the guise of compassion, receive less care so they can "die with dignity" or some other excuse masking passive euthanasia.

There are two types of euthanasia: active and passive. Active euthanasia refers to when action is taken to end a life, for example, a lethal injection. Passive euthanasia is when a person dies prematurely because of having all medicines, food, and water removed (for the sake of reasons such as saving money or urging "quality of life" instead of "pro-life" treatment).

Too often, patients choose to stop fighting for life due to depression. These patients need additional help from loved ones and medical treatment. Such patients could actually live longer or even improve with compassionate care.

In the guise of compassion, helpless elderly and disabled patients are told: "It's better to die than live a poor quality life." But such pat answers disregard the sanctity of life. It pushes aside the idea of trying available treatment options and the possibility of improvement. There are still many compassionate, caring members in the medical profession and we applaud their hard work and commitment. In fact, several of our friends and our own dad are in the field of medicine. Sadly, too often our overall healthcare system has a disturbing environment.

In response, *Unite the USA* urges physicians to remember this part of the Hippocratic Oath: "Above all, I must not play at God. I will remember that I do not treat a fever chart, a cancerous growth, but a sick human being, whose illness may affect the person's family and economic stability."

Euthanasia and abortion share something in common: They

sacrifice lives to the altar of convenience for others. But God loves the people who sinned. He offers forgiveness and freedom through Jesus! (Come to Jesus. He is the only Way to Heaven. If using the e-book, learn more by clicking <u>here</u>.)

CHAPTER THIRTEEN

Guard the Elderly

Guarding the Gift of Life from Birth to Unhurried Death

"...he who does not use his endeavors to heal himself
is brother to him who commits suicide."
–Psalm 18:9

Now is the time to fight for life by bowing down and standing up for
the defenseless! May we all apply Proverbs 31:8 (NLT): "Speak up
for those who cannot speak for themselves; ensure justice for those
being crushed."

In the following article, Nancy Valko, RN does just that. It is
difficult to address this issue so briefly which is why we are honored
to share a riveting article by Mrs. Valko which was featured in *Voices*
magazine. She is a nurse of over 40 years and a spokeswoman for
the National Association of Pro-life Nurses. The following article
appeared as "Then and Now: The Descent of Ethics":

*I feel blessed to have grown up and become a nurse in the era
of TV programs like Marcus Welby, MD, Ben Casey, and*

Medical Center. I couldn't wait to be part of such a noble profession and I proudly recited the "Florence Nightingale Pledge," the nursing equivalent of the Hippocratic Oath, at my graduation from a Catholic nursing school in 1969. Written in 1893 and named in honor of nurse/hero Florence Nightingale, the pledge reads:

I solemnly pledge myself before God and in the presence of this assembly, to pass my life in purity and to practice my profession faithfully. I will abstain from whatever is deleterious and mischievous, and will not take or knowingly administer any harmful drug. I will do all in my power to maintain and elevate the standard of my profession, and will hold in confidence all personal matters committed to my keeping and all family affairs coming to my knowledge in the practice of my calling. With loyalty will I endeavor to aid the physician in his work, and devote myself to the welfare of those committed to my care.

Forty-three years later, I still subscribe to those simple but powerful principles but the healthcare world around me has changed dramatically. On the plus side, I have witnessed the great advances in treating illnesses, pain, etc. However, on the minus side, I have witnessed an increasing rejection of traditional ethics that has turned the world I knew upside-down in so many ways. In 1969, I could never have imagined that the crime of abortion would be declared a constitutional right or that euthanasia in the guise of "physician assisted suicide" would become legal in any state. And could any of us ever have imagined a time when a US president would try to force even Catholic healthcare institutions into violating their conscience rights?

These changes did not happen overnight and neither were

they the result of new scientific discoveries. The tragedy is that this all began with small, deliberate steps.

Contraception and Abortion

In 1965, the American College of Obstetricians and Gynecologists (ACOG) redefined conception from the union of sperm and egg to "the implantation of a fertilized ovum," allowing hormones - like those in the Pill - that can interfere with implantation to be classified as contraceptive rather than potentially abortifacient. Eventually, this opened the door not only to widespread acceptance of artificial contraception but also later developments such as abortifacient "morning after" pills, embryonic stem cell research, and in vitro fertilization (IVF).

Unsurprisingly, abortion itself was legalized a mere eight years after the ACOG redefinition of conception when the stage was already set for a pervasive contraceptive mentality making childbearing merely a "choice." Now, we not only have abortion celebrated as a right but also infertile couples who want to adopt having to compete with same-sex couples for a smaller and smaller pool of available children to love and raise. Some desperate infertile couples resort to IVF, artificial insemination, or surrogate motherhood. Today, unborn babies themselves routinely have to pass "quality control" prenatal tests to escape abortion. And just recently, two parents won almost $3 million in a "wrongful birth" lawsuit because they claimed that they would have aborted their daughter with Down syndrome if the prenatal tests had been accurate.

Moreover, according to two ethicists writing in a recent article in the Journal of Medical Ethics, even a newborn without disabilities does not necessarily have any right to live. Ethicists Alberto Giubilini and Francesca Minerva baldly state that "what we call 'after-birth abortion' *(killing a newborn) should be permissible in all the cases where abortion is, including cases where the newborn is not disabled." This, they argue, should be permissible because, like a fetus, the newborn is only a "potential person."*

Organ Donation
In 1968, an ad hoc committee at Harvard Medical School issued a report defining a type of irreversible coma as a new criterion for death, stating that "[t]he burden is great on patients who suffer permanent loss of intellect, on their families, on the hospitals, and on those in need of hospital beds already occupied by these comatose patients" and the "[o]bsolete criteria for the definition of death can lead to controversy in obtaining organs for transplantation."

Since then, all 50 states have adopted laws adding brain death to the definition of death but each hospital can determine its own, often widely varying, criteria for what counts as brain death.

When brain death did not provide enough organ donations to transplant, some ethicists and doctors devised a new way of obtaining organs. Now, we have non-heart-beating organ donation (aka donation after cardiac death) for people who do not meet the brain death definition and doctors like Robert Truog, who argues that the traditional "dead donor rule" before organ transplantation should be eliminated in favor of taking organs from living patients on life support with "valid consent for both withdrawing treatment and organ donation."

In a final step, doctors in Belgium have already combined euthanasia with organ donation. Could this happen here? Just last year, the New York Times published an article from a death row inmate in Oregon arguing for the right to donate his organs after his own capital punishment by lethal injection, and started an organization promoting this for other prisoners.

The "Right To Die" and Euthanasia

The 1970s brought the invention of "living wills" and the Euthanasia Society of America changed its name to the Society for the Right to Die. The so-called "right to die" movement received a real boost when the parents of Karen Quinlan, a 21-year-old woman considered "vegetative" after a probable drug overdose, "won" the right to remove her ventilator with the support of many prominent Catholic theologians. Karen continued to live 10 more years with a feeding tube, much to the surprise and dismay of some ethicists. Shortly after the Quinlan case, California passed the first "living will" law.

Originally, "living wills" only covered refusal of life-sustaining treatment for imminently dying people. There was some suspicion about this allegedly innocuous document and, here in Missouri, "living will" legislation only passed when "right to die" advocates agreed to a provision exempting food and water from the kinds of treatment to be refused.

But, it wasn't long before the parents of Missouri's Nancy Cruzan, who was also said to be in a "vegetative" state, "won" the right to withdraw her feeding tube despite her not being terminally ill or even having a "living will." The case was appealed to the US Supreme Court, which upheld Missouri law requiring "clear and convincing evidence" that Nancy Cruzan would want her feeding tube removed, but, in the end, a local judge allowed the feeding tube to be removed. Shortly after Nancy's slow death from dehydration, Senators John Danforth and Patrick Moynihan proposed the Patient Self-Determination Act (never voted upon but became law under budget *reconciliation), which required all institutions to offer all patients information on "living wills" and other advance directives. Since then, such directives evolved to include not only the so-called "vegetative" state and feeding tubes but virtually any other condition a person specifies as worse than death and any medical care considered life-sustaining when that person is deemed unable to communicate.*

But has this choice become an illusion? The last several years have also seen the rise of so-called futility policies and even futility laws in Texas that can override patient or family decisions to continue treatment on the basis that doctors and/or ethicists know best.

In the early 1990s, Jack Kevorkian went public with his first assisted suicide and the "right to die" debate took yet another direction. By the end of the decade, Oregon became the first state to allow physician-assisted suicide. At first, the law was portrayed as necessary for terminally ill people with allegedly unrelievable pain. Within a short time, though, it was reported that "according to their physicians, the patients requested assistance with suicide because of concern about loss of autonomy and control of bodily functions, not because of concern about inadequate control of pain or financial loss."

In 2008, Washington became the next state to legalize assisted suicide and in 2009, Montana's state Supreme Court declared that it was not against public policy for a doctor to assist the suicide of a competent terminally ill person. Relentless efforts to legalize assisted suicide in other states have failed so far, but many euthanasia proponents support terminal sedation as a stopgap alternative to assisted suicide for the present. Ominously, just last year assisted suicide activist and terminal sedation advocate Dr.

Timothy Quill was named president-elect of the American Academy of Hospice and Palliative Medicine (AAHPM).

In just the last few months, popular health expert Dr. Mehmet Oz voiced his support for physician-assisted suicide on his TV show and Dr. Phil McGraw hosted a segment on his widely seen TV show featuring a Canadian woman who wanted her adult disabled children to die by lethal injection. Ironically, the mother, along with former Kevorkian lawyer Geoffrey Feiger, argued that removing their feeding tubes was an "inhumane" way to end the lives of the adult children. Tragically, when the studio audience was polled, 90% were in favor of lethal injections for the disabled adults.

The Challenge Ahead

After 43 years, I don't miss the starched nursing uniforms and glass IV bottles of my youth but I certainly do miss the idealism and ethical unity that I shared with my colleagues during that time.

Back then, Catholic nursing education like mine added a level of ministry to our efforts but, Catholic or not, we all shared the common goal of providing the very best health care for every patient regardless of age, socioeconomic status, or condition.

But now, in capitulation to the new ideal of "choice," we doctors and nurses find ourselves ostracized from our professional organizations for being "politically incorrect" when we oppose abortion and stand up for discrimination-free medical care for the disabled. We are warned not be "judgmental" when a terminally ill person asks to die. At the same time, we see our conscience rights being legally dismantled with excuses such as "Doctors, nurses and pharmacists choose professions that put patients' rights first. If they foresee that priority becoming problematic for them, they should choose another profession."

This did not happen overnight but rather by small and ever deepening steps. The result has not been a more compassionate and just society but rather a culture with a false sense of power and entitlement. We have been seduced into believing not only that we deserve control over having or not having children but also the degree of perfection of those chosen children. We think we deserve a life in which the seriously ill or disabled don't financially or emotionally burden us. We think we deserve to decide when our own lives are not worth living, and have a right to be painlessly dispatched by a medical person. And we desperately but ultimately futilely want to believe that our actions and attitudes will not have terrible consequences.

It will take all of us openly and constantly challenging this culture of death to restore the traditional respect for life that protects all our lives.

Wow, that was an extremely heart-stirring, thought-provoking article! Now, let's get to the point. The action point:

ACTION POINT: Nancy Valko's preceding article pairs well with this list to help you fight the "right to die" lie and take action now:

1. The National Right to Life and the Alliance Defense Fund are committed to helping you and your family prepare an "advance directive" that will ensure your pro-life healthcare wishes are observed, even under the most difficult circumstances. Defend yourself against anti-life methods that are currently practiced in the medical community. If using the e-book, click here to learn more about the **Will to Live** Campaign.
2. If using the e-book, click here to download your free Will to

Live wallet card. Keep it in your wallet for easy access in case of an emergency.

3. Elect public officials who are pro-life. We need more men and women in office who believe that life should be protected - from the moment of conception to natural death.

4. Learn more about anti-euthanasia sources, disability rights, and pro-life helps at Terri's Life & Hope Network. (It is Terri Schiavo's organization founded by her brother, Bobby Schindler.) If using the e-book, click here for more information.

5. Share the Hippocratic Oath. Sadly, too many doctors discredit the elderly, unborn, and disabled and they do not try as hard to save them. These individuals should be reminded that they took the Hippocratic Oath - which is strongly pro-life.

CHAPTER FOURTEEN

Secrets from Our Founding Fathers

"The only thing necessary for the triumph of
evil is for good men to do nothing."
- **Edmund Burke**

As we consider the secrets of our Founding Fathers, let us pause and remember another leader in another time of history: Daniel. In an attempt to take him down as a leader in the government of the day, various politicians plotted and found a way to make Daniel disobey an anti-Biblical law made by what one might call an "executive order" by the ruler of the land, King Darius. The entire reason for the law was for the corrupt politicians to gain power and for God's followers to be oppressed by ousting Daniel from his powerful position in government.

The law restricted prayer. The law commanded the people to pay homage to government instead of God. Daniel, meanwhile, was 80 years old and a very well-respected leader who had done great things for the people. His reaction to the anti-God law would be pivotal in how the people would respond.

Daniel refused to change his allegiance from God to government.

He prayed. Take a look at how he responded in spite of having his very life threatened: "When Daniel knew that the document had been signed, he went to his house where he had windows in his upper chamber open toward Jerusalem. He got down on his knees three times a day and prayed and gave thanks before his God, as he had done previously" (Daniel 6:10, ESV).

Tremendous obedience revealed his deepest alliance. He chose to maintain his Godly behavior even at risk of losing the government's favor. He knew he would be seen by the government, monitoring his activities and waiting for a chance to pounce upon him. Yet he remained resolute because he knew God's ways are absolute truth.

Being thrown into the lion's den for praying to the Lord was 80 year old Daniel's reward. Yet he survived and then thrived because God's ways and laws exceed anything that human beings can conjure. Americans would do well to emulate Daniel's courage to stand up and bow down in order to lift high the Name of the Lord.

In America, many leaders are acting like they have the power to determine the divine. Laws are being passed that do not pass God's standards. America, we need His values. We can't make up our own code of ethics. We are the creation...not the Creator. His ways are higher than our ways. He loves like no other! He reigns supremely, sovereignly, perfectly... And we desperately need revival in our hearts.

You see, like it or not, God remains God. And we, as Christians, must stand up for what is right...just like Daniel. (Read his story in Daniel 6.)

We need to be like Daniel. We need to obey God and care more about what He says than what people say. No more PC. No more compromises "to win" elections, etc. No more.

Today, we challenge our friends and ourselves. Do what God wants us to do. Shrug off the burden of false pride. Let's run the race with Christ as our Coach and Supreme King!

When we start pointing fingers to blame others, we need God's grace to stop us from becoming like what we hate. One quote really reached us: "Usually when we pray for revival, we're thinking about the bad guys, and we're telling God to 'sic 'em.' Little do we realize that revival begins with us, the people of God. As a matter of fact, we've got a suggestion for those who want revival: Don't pray for revival. Just repent of all known sin, do everything you're supposed to do, give God all—not part, but all—your time, and you'll experience revival" (Dr. Elmer Towns and Douglas Porter).

It's up to each of us to turn to God and not let government determine what is right and wrong. Like many of our Founding Fathers, we need to embrace Biblical values and live with courage in Christ.

The secret to our Founding Father's success was prayer and courage to obey God's Word –against all odds. They embraced the Ten Commandments. They fought for justice. They weren't perfect, but they sought help from the perfect One: God Himself.

Fast and Pray

Flashback: Did you know that our country used to have national fast and pray days? On March 16, 1776, the Continental Congress declared a national fast. **You see, contrary to liberal thought, we have a right to believe that this country was founded on Judeo-Christian beliefs.** You don't have to be quiet about your opinion while liberal courses in schools promote other beliefs.

Shortly before the Revival of 1857, Congress included an amazing declaration: **"The great, vital, and conservative element in our system is the belief of our people in the pure doctrines and the divine truths of the Gospel of Jesus Christ."**-*Journal of the House of the Representatives of the United States of America* [8]

You see, while many liberals like to dismiss Christians who claim

---

8   (Washington, DC: Cornelius Wendell, 1855), 34th Cong., 1st Sess., p. 354, January 23, 1856; see also: Lorenzo D. Johnson, *Chaplains of the General Government With Objections to their Employment Considered* (New York: Sheldon, Blakeman & Co., 1856), p. 35, quoting from the House Journal, Wednesday, January 23, 1856, and B. F. Morris, *The Christian Life and Character of the Civil Institutions of the United States* (Philadelphia: George W. Childs, 1864), p. 328.

that our Founding Fathers were mere deists, many leaders and heroes of the American Revolution were, indeed, Christians. We particularly appreciate the way in "Founding Faith: Christians in America", by Focus on the Family Issue Analysts:

The Founding Fathers counted on the active engagement of Christians in the country they were forming -- because they understood that morals and religion were necessary for the new form of government they were establishing.

America's Founders would have no argument with that. In fact, they were counting on Christian citizens as the backbone of the republic.

"There was a consensus among the Founders that religion was indispensable to a system of republican self-government," says Daniel Dreisbach, professor of law, justice and American society at American University. In order to have self-government, "the Founders looked to religion (and morality informed by religious faith) to provide the internal moral compass that would prompt citizens to behave in a disciplined manner and thereby promote social order and political stability."[1]

The Founders themselves said this often, in their own inimitable words.

"Our constitution was made only for a moral and religious people. It is wholly inadequate for the government of any other," John Adams declared in a message to the Officers of the First Brigade of the Third Division of the Militia of Massachusetts, October 11, 1798.

"Religion and virtue are the only foundations, not only of republicanism and all free government, but of social felicity under all governments and in all the combinations of human society." - John Adams (Letter to Dr. Benjamin Rush, August 28, 1811)

"We ought to be no less persuaded that the propitious smiles of heaven can never be expected on a nation that disregards the eternal rules of order and right which heaven itself has ordained." George Washington, Farewell Address, September 19, 1796.

On December 22, 1820, Daniel Webster summed it up in a nutshell: "Whatever makes men good Christians, makes them good citizens." (Many more quotes are available at WallBuilders.com.)

There's a myth in some circles that the Founders weren't primarily

Christians but Deists — believers in a God who wound up the universe like a watch, then left it to run on its own. But while that describes a handful of them, it doesn't fit the vast majority.

Of the 55 Framers of the Constitution, "with no more than five exceptions, they were orthodox members of one of the established congregations," wrote the late University of Dallas historian M.E. Bradford. "References made by the Framers to Jesus Christ as Redeemer and Son of God ... are commonplace in their private papers, correspondence and public remarks — and in the early records of their lives."

And they did a lot more than talk about their faith.

"The variety of surviving Christian witness in the papers and sayings of the Framers is indeed astonishing. Elias Boudinot of New Jersey was heavily involved in Christian missions and was the founder of the American Bible Society. Roger Sherman ... was a ruling elder of his church. Richard Bassett rode joyfully with his former slaves to share in the enthusiasm of their singing on the way to Methodist camp meetings.... John Dickinson of Delaware wrote persuasive letters to youthful friends conserving the authority of Scripture and the soundness of Christian evidences. ... both James Madison and Alexander Hamilton regularly led their households in the observance of family prayers."

Readers, there's more: Guess what? An awakening happened in the decades leading up to the Revolution. In history, it's entitled, "The Great Awakening". You've read a lot of what we've had to say. So here is a quote that will make anyone sit up straighter in attention:

> "I believe that no one can read the history of our country without realizing the good book [the Bible] and the spirit of the Savior which we have from the beginning been our guiding genius. Whether we look at the first charter of Virginia, or the charter of New England, or the charter of Massachusetts Bay, or the fundamental orders of Connecticut, the same objective

is present, a Christian land governed by Christian principles...I believe the entire Bill of Rights came into being because of the knowledge of our forefathers had of the Bible and their belief in it. Freedom of belief, of expression, of assembly, of petition, the dignity of the individual, the sanctity of the home, equal justice under the law, and the reservation of the powers to the people...I would like to believe that we are living today in the spirit of the Christian religion. I would also like to believe that as long as we do, no great harm can come to our country."

-Earl Warren, former Chief Justice of the Supreme Court

The preceding quote came not from a conservative, but from a liberal! How our conditions have worsened since his 1954 speech, as reported in Time Magazine. Yet the point remains the same: America was founded and is intended to be a Christian nation. This does not mean that we espouse a theocracy. (The only theocracy to come is that of Jesus Christ's return to reign.) Rather, it means we desire to honor our Heavenly Father and promote a moral, God-honoring society embracing Christianity as our moral compass.

In essence, like the Founding Fathers, we must welcome God's presence and we must work hard to protect our freedom.

CHAPTER FIFTEEN

Victory Guaranteed

"But the path of the [uncompromisingly] just and righteous
is like the light of dawn, that shines more and more (brighter
and clearer) until [it reaches its full strength and glory in]
the perfect day [to be prepared]." **–Proverbs 4:18, AMP**

Little wonder that some people today feel discouraged. But we can be
encouraged as we realize that every generation feels like its era looms
the darkest and hardest. For Christians, we know we have the Light
of the world on our side. We know that nothing done for Christ will
ever be wasted. Our victory remains secure in Christ. Yes, it can be
challenging sometimes. Yes, the battle can feel overwhelming. But, if
God is for us, who can be against us? We can do our part and know
that God will see and reward us for loving our neighbor, being faithful
to the Lord, etc.

Yes, some say our country's downturn feels like a David and
Goliath situation. But people have always felt that way about their
own particular era in history. So let's remember this when we feel like
we're facing a giant: With God's help, David won! It is amazing what

the average American can accomplish for our country! It's as simple as the ABC's:

> **A: Act.** Don't just talk. Act. Have your own prayer meetings before attending town hall meetings, always vote - even in primaries and mid-term elections, and call/write your Congressman about your concerns. Educate your children about the Christian history of American government. (Through education, you will discover more ways to make your voice heard.) Be aware of the news and be involved in influencing policies. (The American Family Association and Liberty Counsel are great organizations that help people stay informed.)

> **B: Be bold (and respectful). Contact legislators and be ready to express your position while backing it up with facts, respectful firmness, and faith.**

> **C: Connect.** Connect with your Congressmen and women enough that they know your name. Often, their offices correspond more than you'd expect! Meet your representatives in person and establish a rapport. And, of course, one option is to connect with them on Facebook and share with your friends via such posts. (Facebook has its disadvantages, but one advantage is to network with fellow conservatives and stay alert to goings on that the secular media ignore. For example, our FB page, Unite the USA, includes original Founding Fathers' quotes, Scripture, prayer, action alerts, info on other pro-family/pro-faith sites.)

How to Help Young People Become Voters

Young people become voters. How can families educate and encourage their kids to be active citizens? We advocate the tips below:

1. **Encourage young people to talk with veterans and learn about their experiences and sacrifices on the battlefield and home front.** If America's youth would gain an understanding about the great sacrifices made to keep them free, they would appreciate our country and our veterans.

2. **Educate the young people in your life about the wealth of opportunities and advantages that are available in America.** Watch documentaries about third world countries and countries under tyrannical law. Or, if possible, visit a less privileged country. That way, America's youth will value freedom and opportunities in a new way.

3. **Have young people visit historical landmarks. It will make America's history "come to life".** That way, they will appreciate our nation's heritage on a personal level.

4. **Encourage young people to read the <u>Declaration of Independence</u> and the <u>U.S. Constitution</u>.** Explain the meaning of each document and allow them to appreciate the documents for themselves.

5. **Help America's youth become active citizens.** Show them how they can make a difference in America. Educate the young people in your life about government practices and take them to political meetings and to your State Capitol.

Register to Vote

Do your part and vote! <u>Click here</u> and make sure that you are registered to vote for the next election. Use the voter look-up tool and the register to vote section to make sure that you are ready to exercise your right to vote.

Let's work hard, persevere, and help one American at a time. We must hoist high the torch and stand for faith and freedom. Like 9/11 hero Todd Beamer, we all need to say, "Let's roll!" With God as our guide, we can unite the USA to fight for freedoms today so that

America will stay bright for tomorrow! **Remember, don't get down on our country: Get down on your knees and look up!**

ACTION POINT: Share the above information with grade school students. They need to know the truth. And here's an interesting fact to share: Francis Scott Key, author of the "Star Spangled Banner", put it well: "[M]ay I always hear that you are following the guidance of that blessed Spirit that will lead you into all truth, leaning on that Almighty arm that has been extended to deliver you, trusting only in the only Savior, and going on in your way to Him rejoicing." And, as we share this information, may we all remember this: "I can do all things through Christ who strengthens me" (Philippians 4:13, NKJV).

+100 Ways to "Take Action Now"

Instead of letting ad campaigns reign and distract, start looking for ways to support America. Here are dozens and dozens of ways to do so:

1. Resist the urge to trust the media. **Understand for yourself why we became a country.** Far too many Americans have no clue what the Declaration of Independence even says. **Take time to read it.** It's not a long document and it is a fascinating read. The Declaration of Independence was a statement adopted by the Continental Congress on July 4, 1776. In the midst of the American Revolution, it announced that the thirteen American colonies regarded themselves as independent states (no longer a part of the British Empire). Primarily written by Thomas Jefferson, the Declaration of Independence details grievances against King George III and Great Britain regarding their abuse of power. If using the e-book, click here to read the Declaration of Independence.

2. **Read and re-read the U.S. Constitution until you can get a basic grasp on its truths.** On September 17, 1787, eleven years after the Declaration of Independence was written, the Constitution was adopted by the Constitutional Convention in Philadelphia, Pennsylvania. Our Constitution has provided a stable, practical guide for governing. The underlying principles of the Constitution were gathered by the delegates from years of

careful study of governments and political thinkers, and also from the failed lessons learned from the failed Confederation. Limited government, separation of powers, and checks and balances are major themes in our Constitution. The Constitutional framers forged a working balance with these principles that has provided our country with liberty, order, and an enduring charter. If using the e-book, <u>click here</u> to read the U.S. Constitution.

3. **Discover, claim, and defend your rights!** Many people do not realize that the Bill of Rights consists of the first ten amendments of the Constitution. James Madison introduced these amendments on July 21, 1789 and they were ratified on December 15, 1791. The Constitution and the Bill of Rights made liberty secure. (i.e. The First Amendment insures five freedoms: religion, speech, press, assembly, and petition.) The amendments illustrate the principle of limited government. For example, Congress cannot establish any church or denomination as a state-sponsored church. People are free to worship as they choose. Read the Bill of Rights <u>here</u>.

4. **Be able to answer this: What did the Founding Fathers intend?** Acclaimed by Thomas Jefferson as "the best commentary on the principles of government which ever was written," the <u>Federalist Papers</u> make a powerful case for power-sharing between state and federal authorities. The Federalist Papers were written by "Publius" the pseudonym for Alexander Hamilton, John Jay, and James Madison. They were a collection of 85 articles promoting the ratification of the U.S. Constitution. The Federalist Papers detail the intent of the U.S. Constitution as seen by the Founding Fathers. Read the Federalist Papers to learn what was thought and believed by the men who helped shape our country.

5. **Oh say, can you sing the National Anthem?** "The Star-Spangled Banner" is our nation's National Anthem. The lyrics come from a poem written in 1814 by a 35-year-old lawyer, Francis Scott Key. He was inspired to write it after watching the bombardment of Fort McHenry during the War of 1812. "The Star-Spangled Banner" was officially declared as our National Anthem in 1931.

Learn the <u>lyrics</u> of the National Anthem. As a way to show respect for our country and freedom, always stand and place your right hand over your heart. If using the e-book, <u>click here</u> to watch Stacie Ruth sing our National Anthem.

6. **Pledge allegiance to the flag!** The Pledge of Allegiance of the United States is a way for citizens to express their dedication and love for their country and freedom. Through the years, it has been modified four times. Most recently, the words "under God" were added in 1954. The introduction of "under God" in the 1950s was done during the Cold War, as a way to differentiate the U.S. from the concept of Communist state atheism. Here is the Pledge of Allegiance: "I pledge allegiance to the flag of the United States of America, and to the republic for which it stands, one nation under God, indivisible, with liberty and justice for all."

7. **Pass the torch of liberty.** Take time to teach your children and grandchildren about the greatness of our God and country. Without you, how will they learn? Your personal touch, time, and attention are effective in encouraging children to love faith and freedom. No school, group, or TV/computer program can replace the impact that you personally can have on our next generation. Visit your local library or bookstore to find resources about our country, government, and history. Have your kids meet our nation's heroes in your community.

8. **Put your guard up about too much government. Be aware of current events.** Be aware about what is happening in the news and in the federal and state legislatures. Do not assume that government programs with nice sounding names are safe and for the good of the people. (Sometimes the most dangerous bills have great sounding titles.) It's easy to keep up with current events through the radio, TV, newspapers, and online tools. It's simply up to you to take advantage of those accessible resources.

9. **Voting does count!** Over 50% of eligible voters do not make the effort to vote. Don't be part of that group. It's easy yet very important to vote. You do not need to stand in line at the polls.

Instead, vote via an absentee ballot. Contact your auditor's office to request an absentee ballot. In fact, throughout history there have been many elections when only a hand full of votes made all of the difference.

10. **Visit historical landmarks to make our history 'come to life'.** It reinforces the fact that our past is real. For example, visit your state capitol building, presidential libraries, battle sites, or any other historical landmarks in your area that interest you. Seeing places where our government works or where history happened makes history and government text books much more interesting, real, and applicable.

11. **Lawmakers serve you. Request meetings with your lawmakers.** Many state and federal legislators regularly tour their constituencies and hold town hall meetings. For example, it is widely known that in Iowa, Senator Chuck Grassley tours all 99 counties every year. Make the time and effort to meet with your public servants to hear what they have to say about current news and legislation. **Our leaders need to hear from you.**

12. **Pray for our nation.** America was founded by God-fearing men and women. 2 Chronicles 7:14 (AMP) says, "If My people, who are called by My name, shall humble themselves, pray, seek, crave, and require of necessity My face and turn from their wicked ways, then will I hear from heaven, forgive their sin, and heal their land." Prayer is powerful. Learn more about our prayer group at http://www.prayingpals.org/ .

13. **Interview members of the Greatest Generation while there's time.** Ask your church to recommend someone for you to visit. Ask your librarian. Or e-mail a nursing home. Ask them what they did. Personal testimonies will educate and inspire you more than you can envision.

14. **Be resourceful** – The Greatest Generation would reuse their resources. For example, our grandparents saved certain plastic bags (i.e. bread bags) and used them for other items (i.e. to cover brownies).

15. **Respect our military.** Fly a flag. Visit wounded veterans. Donate to pro-veteran organizations.

16. **Parents –not government– must parent America's children.** Teach your kids why America is great!

17. **Get in the kitchen!** Did you know that chocolate chip cookies originated in America? Spend time with your kids and bake some together. It's a fun project for everyone – especially kids!

18. **Spend time together at the family table.** It is so important to connect and regularly spend time together as a family. Simply eating dinner together each night can make a big difference in your family. On a larger scale, consider these words from President Ronald Reagan: "All great change in America begins at the dinner table."

19. **Try making something instead of buying it.** Example: Try baking bread for fun. Even if it doesn't turn out perfectly, you'll appreciate bread so much more.

20. **Go to church regularly and take it out with you to your community.** Invite a friend along and ride together for fun.

21. **Have regular family get-togethers with extended family, if possible. Play patriotic music in the background once in a while.**

22. **Write handwritten letters to loved ones. And tell them you love them.**

23. **Live without something that takes away from family time.** And instead enjoy every day life as a family –not just on weekends. Live it up with your family and friends! Invite your neighbors over. Do chores together instead of apart, if possible. Guard family time. Embrace God-given life today and hope for tomorrow!

24. **Honor the elderly instead of viewing them as extras.** Encourage kids to respect the elderly and include your elderly loved ones/ friends as often as possible. Ask them to share lessons they've learned.

25. **Instead of reading a self-help book, help somebody else in your neighborhood.**

26. **Contact Congress** and use our helpful contact information at the back of the book.

27. **Send letters** to editors, bloggers, and all media.

28. **Defend yourself against anti-life methods** that are currently practiced in the medical community. The National Right to Life and the Alliance Defense Fund are committed to helping you and your family prepare an "advance directive" that will ensure your pro-life healthcare wishes are observed, even under the most difficult circumstances. If using the e-book, click here to learn more about the **Will to Live** Campaign.

29. If using the e-book, **click here to download your free Will to Live wallet card.** Keep it in your wallet for easy access in case of an emergency.

30. **Elect public officials who are pro-life.** We need more men and women in office who believe that life should be protected - from the moment of conception to natural death.

31. **Learn more about anti-euthanasia sources, disability rights, and pro-life helps at Terri's Life & Hope Network.** (It is Terri Schiavo's organization founded by her brother, Bobby Schindler.) If using the e-book, click here for more information.

32. **Read the Hippocratic Oath.** Sadly, too many doctors discredit the elderly, unborn, and disabled and they do not try as hard to save them. These individuals should be reminded that they took the **Hippocratic Oath** - which is strongly pro-life.

33. **Send a thank-you card or e-mail a caring note to a veteran in your life.** Or, if you don't know a veteran, contact a local care facility and inquire. You could send a card addressed to all veterans at a nursing home. Many nursing homes/hospitals offer to deliver e-mails to residents. (Of course, cards are more colorful and inspirational than e-mails. But e-mails are far better than nothing!)

34. **Call a veteran and thank him/her for serving.** Often, a short call sheds lasting light onto a veteran's soul. Many feel forgotten. We can flip that fact inside out!

35. **Send flowers.** We know this sounds morbid, but there is truth to

this: Rather than wait for the funeral, we need to send the flowers now. Plus, they do not have to be big bouquets.

36. **Visit a veteran. Or take a veteran out to dinner.** Following their initial return home from war, many haven't savored a special meal given in honor of their service.

37. **Don't forget our young veterans.** They deserve an e-card, note, or gift, too. Our courageous college-age young men and women face countless challenges. Our efforts can combat depression induced by combat. Web sites such as www.americasupportsyou. mil/americasupportsyou/index.aspx and www.amillionthanks. org serve as extremely easy media through which to convey thanks to our valorous veterans.

38. **Send a serviceman or woman a care package.** It means so much to them to receive something from home. Send items like phone cards, photos from home, DVDs, CD, etc. See more details in Chapter 1.

39. Consider the V.O.T.E.R. points from Chapter 8: **View the country from an eagle's eye and not from a feelings-only, close-range perspective.** If we don't risk hurting misguided people's feelings, we risk hurting our country. Do it respectfully, kindly, and prayerfully. Put aside temporary feelings of discomfort as you share facts about your candidate. The foundations of our country are at stake!

40. **Overcome apathy. An active minority overtakes an inactive majority.** Today, apathy runs rampant. Some Christians snivel, cross their arms, and refuse to cast votes for less than ideal candidates. "Why vote when my first choice didn't make it?" People depend on others to stand up for their values. Yet, if everyone thought that way, no one would stand and the country would fall.

41. **Research the candidates.** Who is pro-life, pro-elderly, and pro-small government? Learn more about candidates and their stances by reading a voter scorecard from the FRC and visit www. ivotevalues.org.

42. **Support candidates who will defend the Second Amendment.** The right to bear arms is critical in a free society. When it comes to 'gun control', think of it as 'victim disarmament'. Our Founding Fathers knew what they were doing. For example, Thomas Jefferson said, "The strongest reason for the people to retain the right to keep and bear arms is, as a last resort, to protect themselves against tyranny in government." (Think about that statement!)

43. **Employ the "friendly, firm, and fair" logic** when conveying why you want other people to vote for your candidate.

44. **Pray before you vote.** Then pray for fellow voters. And pray for all candidates -even those of the opposition. (Changed hearts equal changed votes.)

45. **Put up signs** in your yard, on Facebook and Twitter, on your car, etc. And actually talk about it. (**Again, fear of getting unfriendly responses only increases our country's chances to fall and fail.**)

46. **Temper your temper.** Discover the effective results of rational, educational discussion. Be above dirty politics. Stay calm and respectful when in a challenging discussion. You will stand out.

47. **Energize your friends, co-workers, grocery store clerks, etc.** Positive, respectful persuasion quickly ripples thru a nation until it builds into a wave!

48. **Refuse fear.** Silent conservatives, let's emerge from shyness and politely, positively vocalize truth. Frankly, a fear of hurting feelings hurts our country.

49. **Use the ABCs of Patriotism: A: Act. Don't just talk. Act.** Have your own prayer meetings before attending town hall meetings, always vote - even in primaries and mid-term elections, and call/write your Congressman about your concerns. Educate your children about the Christian history of American government. (Through education, you will discover more ways to make your voice heard.) Be aware of the news and be involved in influencing policies. (The American Family Association and Liberty Counsel are great organizations that help people stay informed.) And always vote – even in primaries and mid-term elections.

50. **B: Be bold (and respectful).** Contact legislators and be ready to express your position while backing it up with facts, respectful firmness, and faith. Be aware of the news and understand what is happening in Congress and the state legislature. For example, if you are aware of legislation that is either in committee or coming up for a vote, you will be able to contact the appropriate offices to express your opinion and back it up with facts.

51. **C: Connect kindly. Connect with your Congressmen and women.** Often, their offices correspond more than you'd expect! Meet your representatives and establish a rapport. And, of course, connect with them on Facebook and share with your friends.

52. **Encourage young people to talk with veterans and learn about their experiences and sacrifices on the battlefield and home front.** If America's youth would gain an understanding about the great sacrifices made to keep them free, they would appreciate our country and our veterans.

53. **Educate the young people in your life about the wealth of opportunities and advantages that are available in America.** Watch documentaries about third world countries and countries under tyrannical law. Or, if possible, visit a less privileged country. That way, America's youth will value freedom and opportunities in a new way.

54. **Have young people visit historical landmarks. It will make America's history "come to life".** That way, they will appreciate our nation's heritage on a personal level.

55. **Encourage young people to read the <u>Declaration of Independence</u> and the <u>U.S. Constitution</u>.** Explain the meaning of each document and allow them to appreciate the documents for themselves.

56. **Help America's youth become active citizens.** Show them how they can make a difference in America. Include them in your own civic involvement.

57. **As a way to support the fight for life, support and donate time, money to Christian ministries, and help dissuade potential**

mothers from having abortions. Here are examples of such ministries that aid teenage mothers such as:

i. Bethany Christian Services (http://www.bethany.org/)
ii. Birthright International (www.birthright.org)
iii. Care-Net (https://www.care-net.org/),
iv. Christian Life Resources
    (http://www.christianliferesources.com/)
v. Life Dynamics (http://www.lifedynamics.com/).

58. **Stay aware about current pro-life news thru web sites like www.lifenews.com and www.nrlc.org.**

59. **Don't be afraid to help.** Simply telling a girl not to abort her baby is not enough. You need to give her an alternative. Contact your local problem pregnancy center and ask how you can help. There are always basic needs like housing for the girls, finances, maternity and baby clothes, electrical, carpentry, or maintenance work, etc. You may be able to offer valuable assistance through your business or profession - you'd be surprised how many different needs there are!

60. **Try sidewalk counseling.** It is talking with the girls as they are going in and out of the abortion clinics. This can be very effective, and we've heard many great reports about women changing their minds. The only way you're going to save the child is through the mother. She probably feels frightened, confused, and backed into a corner. Many women aren't really sure abortion is the right thing, but most of them don't know the other options available. Learn more about it from Keith and Melody Green's website at www.lastdaysministries.com

61. If using the e-book, **click here to watch and then share a very informative video about the truth about Planned Parenthood.**

62. **Encourage adoption in your community.**

63. **Watch *October Baby!*** It's a great movie with a compelling prolife story. It includes the message of Jesus' love and forgiveness to women who made the mistake of having an abortion. Be sure to watch *October Baby!*

64. **Talk with your pastor about ways to reach out!**
65. **Inform the general public.** You or your church could buy billboard space and run newspaper ads. Take time to write articles or "letters to the editor," give speeches, write songs, and inform your school.
66. **Inform your friends, family, and church about the truth about abortion.** One great resource is a DVD called *The Gift of Life*. Hosted by former Arkansas Governor Mike Huckabee, the film explores the sanctity of life as a moral issue. It looks at the lives of individuals who were nearly the victims of an abortion, but through God's grace were spared. Be sure to watch and share this film. It could save a life. If using the e-book, click here to order your copy.
67. **Help others learn about embryo adoption.** If using the e-book, click here to visit a helpful web site.
68. **Become CPR certified.** It's simple to learn yet you could save a life. Now that's making a difference! Learn more here.
69. **Spend time with your kids.** Personal attention and interest in your children's education is essential. **Studies show that kids learn better with extra help from their parents.** Whether your children go to public, private, or home school, they need your help, time, and interest in their education. It *does* make a big difference.
70. **Supplement your kids' schooling with extracurricular resources.** There are many great educational books and DVDs available for all ages. Visit the library or look at ChristianBook.com, Answers in Genesis, or Wallbuilders.com for a lot of great resources.
71. **Vote for candidates who support options like homeschooling, school vouchers, etc.** In America, parents should have the right to choose where their children attend school.
72. If using the e-book, **click here to visit the White House web site and view biographies and pictures of America's presidents.**
73. **What would our U.S. President be without our First Ladies?**

If using the e-book, <u>click here</u> to learn about the fascinating ladies who have contributed so much to our heritage.

74. **Discover a selection of excellent resources by Dr. D. James Kennedy and Chuck Colson.** Visit <u>www.truthinaction.org</u> and <u>www.colsoncenter.org</u>.

75. **Listen to a great <u>interview</u> about Presidents' Day with David Barton on Moody Radio.**

76. **Check out this <u>time-line</u> of our Presidents** and see videos, read their biographies, speeches, and view photo galleries. Take advantage of this interactive resource.

77. **We all know that Hollywood tends to promote negative messages in the movies. So, let's do something about it! Write a letter to the Motion Picture Association of America (MPAA).** The MPAA is a strong force in rating movies. It currently does not have absolute rules to determine how a movie should be rated. Politely share your desire to have an absolute film rating system.

Motion Picture Association of America
15503 Ventura Boulevard
Encino, California 91436
E-mail: <u>ContactUs@mpaa.org</u>

78. **Urge your friends and family to write to the MPAA.** The more letters the MPAA receives, the more will be done!

79. **Boycott undesirable motion pictures.** If Hollywood does not receive revenue from distasteful films, it will become financially aware that consumers find unclean movies unappealing. By simply refraining from buying a movie ticket, renting a DVD, and watching inappropriate films on television, you can control Hollywood's content.

80. **Attend the family-friendly movies!** Give Hollywood your support when it makes a great film. Visit <u>www.parentstv.org</u> or <u>www.pluggedinonline.com</u> to read excellent reviews about current movies. There, you can learn details concerning a film's

content. You will be able to discover both positive and negative aspects about films. It is a wonderful tool to use in making your decisions as to whether or not you should attend a movie.

81. Visit **www.unitedformovieaction.com** for more information.

82. **Encourage your family and friends to boycott inappropriate movies.**

83. **Volunteer:** Please prayerfully consider volunteering your time and skills to pro-life organizations (i.e. Right to Life). Please consider making a donation as well.

84. **Be Visible:** Wear a pro-life t-shirt, display a bumper sticker, or whatever you can think of to be responsibly and respectfully visible for the pro-life cause.

85. **Please pray for those who are promoting abortion and euthanasia.** Prayer is powerful and it is crucial in our fight for life.

86. **Be Informed.** Make an effort to know what is going on around you and in the news – locally and nationally.

87. **Learn more about America's Founding Fathers.** Did you know that there were 56 Founding Fathers?

88. **Read.** Is America a Christian nation? Read and share this insightful article here.

89. **Put your patriotism in action.** Contact your Congressman about key issues today.

90. **Call your U.S. Senator today!** Tell your senator about your love for America and express your views on current bills.

91. **Read the "How to Help" section below provided by the Terri Schiavo Foundation:**

92. **Education:** It is important that people understand their state laws as they relate to the withdrawal of ordinary provisions. Many laws have changed or have been amended in recent years and your current advanced directive (or lack of one) might be dangerous under the new laws. We strongly urge all people to carefully read current state laws and to secure legal advice when considering them.

Self-Advocacy: We also encourage people to take proactive measures to ensure that their desires for ordinary care be observed. Considering a health care surrogate, a Protective Medical Decisions Directive along with a Will to Live Directive may be an excellent alternative to the traditional living will.

Community Involvement: Through the internet, public awareness efforts and advocacy for the disabled and elderly, community involvement has a direct and positive impact. Becoming a volunteer is a good way to start.

Get Involved: Throughout Terri's ordeal and her family's attempts to protect her life, many people from across the nation and around the globe offered their help, kindness and friendship. For this, we can never fully express our gratitude...If you are an attorney or in the medical profession and would like to join us, please tell us a little about yourself. One of our site volunteers will be in touch with you as soon as possible. Your information will be kept confidential. E-mail info@lifeandhope.com and visit www.terrisfight.org.

Make A Donation: By making a donation to the Terri Schindler Schiavo Foundation you are helping persons with disabilities, and the incapacitated who are in or potentially facing life-threatening situations. Thank you for enabling us to speak for those who cannot speak for themselves.

93. **Discover how to protect the sanctity of marriage in your state** (especially Iowa) by visiting LetUsVote.com.

94. Billy Graham's web site (www.bgea.org) offers help and resources for those struggling with homosexuality. If using the e-book, click here to find help now.

95. **Remember to pray for our country and our churches as they respond to same-sex "marriage".** And please pray for people who are practicing homosexuality and that they will repent and believe in Jesus. Thank you!

96. **Fight for children's protection:** We believe that marriage is a sacred union between one man and one woman before God. We also believe that the judicial branch should not declare same-sex

"marriage" legal without the approval from the people. Americans should have the right to vote on marriage amendments in their own states. Please take action now to protect the sanctity of marriage in your state. Note the following action points:

97. **Contact your state legislators** and urge them to take the steps necessary to allow the people to vote on a marriage amendment declaring that marriage should be between one man and one woman.

98. **Call or write your governor** and express your desire to add a marriage amendment to your state's Constitution.

99. **Urge your state Senate Majority Leader and Speaker of the House** to allow the legislature to move forward with a marriage amendment.

100. **Play patriotic music from time to time.** Naturally, we recommend our CD, *In God We Still Trust.* ☺

101. **Watch inspiring, patriotic movies** such as *Mr. Smith Goes to Washington* and *Sergeant York.*

102. **Learn about Community in Action**, a grassroots outreach from Truth in Action (Del Tackett's and D. James Kennedy's ministry). It works in local communities to help believers discover God's call on their lives and take action to transform the culture and their communities for Christ. Learn more about it at: <u>www.truthinaction.org</u>.

Appendix I: How to Be Saved

Testimony from Stacie Ruth,

Founder of Praying Pals:
Jesus loves me. Guess what? It's one song from childhood that actually remains real. Yes, it's true! Jesus loves you. And I'm not just a young "idealistic" person. I've seen a lot...including a head-on, fatal accident.

Horrified, I witnessed a head-on collision of a car and helmetless motorcyclist on the highway. But Jesus didn't leave me on the roadside. He held my sister's and my hands as we hovered over an accident victim, a wonderful husband and dad of two. The victim died before paramedics arrived. But we prayed with him and that Jesus would be with him. Now, the accident victim lives in Heaven.

Today, if you were killed in an accident like that, would you enter Heaven?

———————————

Praying Pals founder, Stacie Ruth, and her sister, Carrie Beth, invite you to visit their ministry's site at www.BrightLightMinistry.com.

Be sure to check out the page of resources for hurting hearts and send your prayer requests anytime!

How to Know God's Heavenly Love

Question: How do Stacie Ruth and her sister, Carrie Beth, know they'll go to Heaven?

Answer: It's not because of what they've done or who they are. It's because Jesus lives in them.

Anything good in them is because of Jesus in them. They know God and His love in a personal way. They've followed what God said in His book: the Bible. They invited Jesus to be their Savior and Lord. You, too, can know God. Yes, He really does love you!

Take His Word for it:

- For God so loved the world that He gave His only begotten Son, that whoever believes in Him should not perish but have everlasting life. -John 3:16 (NKJV)
- For all have sinned; all fall short of God's glorious standard.-Rom. 3:23 (NLV)
- For God sent Jesus to take the punishment for our sins and to satisfy God's anger against us. We are made right with God when we believe that Jesus shed his blood, sacrificing his life for us... -Rom. 3:25 (NLV)
- that if you confess with your mouth the Lord Jesus and believe in your heart that God has raised Him from the dead, you will be saved. -Rom. 10:9 (NKJV)

Understand that God loves you with infinite love! God is good, holy and righteous and we fall short of His perfection. So we need a Mediator, Jesus, who lovingly took our punishment for all our mistakes.

Believe that Jesus is God's Son that took your punishment. He took your punishment for all your sins (anti-God ways) and that He rose from the dead for you, _____.

Repent (turn away from) your sins (anti-God ways) and submit yourself to Him as your Lord.

Receive Jesus as your personal Savior and Lord. Talk to God and give your life to Jesus.

Pray from your heart. If it helps, pray something like this:

God,

I understand now...You sent Jesus to share Your love and make it possible for me to be Yours. Please forgive me for all my sins. Jesus, I believe you took my punishment on the cross and that you rose from the dead for me personally. I turn away from doing things "my way" and ask that You rule my life, Jesus. I receive You as my Savior and Lord. I put my trust in You and not in the things I do. I love You.

In Jesus' Name,

Amen.

Welcome into God's family! You are now His! Get connected with a loving, Bible-based church, enjoy the supreme joy of being baptized, and savor the Savior's love forever! Read the Bible. (If you don't have one, start reading the Gospel of John by clicking here.) Also, if you want a Gospel of John, contact our mission at www.brightlightministries.com.

He'll never divorce you. He'll never die. He'll never change. He loves you! Enjoy loving and obeying Jesus and experiencing His love forever and ever! If you'd like prayer or more information, e-mail us anytime.

Appendix II: Quick Quotables

**Stacie and Carrie's quotes on Unite the USA
have been shared thousands of times.
They're quick and to the point. Feel free to use their quotes
in letters to the editor, to Congress, and on social media!**

"It's 'we the people' not 'we the government' and we mustn't forget it!"

"Life, liberty, and justice for all...including yet unborn Americans. Let babies live!"

"The culture that cherishes life thrives. The culture that demeans life dives. Let's promote pro-life, whole-life for every American!"

"There's no separation, we're one nation under God!"

"In politics, it's not just about who is right. It's about what is right... and doing it."

"Make a difference tomorrow by starting something today."

"If everyone thought someone else would take the torch, no one would do it. Never doubt the importance of one American trusting God and stepping up to the plate. Be that American!"

"Some people shrug and say, 'It's just the way it is now.' But it doesn't have to be. Changes begin when hands fold, sin ceases, and hard work ensues."

"If you're reading this, you are a person who once was an unborn baby yet your mom let you live. It's time to cry out for the babies that cannot cry! Pray and act with love for mothers to help them do what's right and let their babies live."

"Why not be an active patriot? Many died for you to be free and vote. They weren't too busy."

"People who hate America should vacate America. America IS beautiful!"

"Being politically incorrect can be totally correct. :)"

"America IS beautiful! No apologies."

"If you're an American, you're blessed!"

"Politicians can't save us. Only God's Son can. (I know that's not PC, but I'm a Christian who loves God more than popularity.)"

"Now is no time to wave the white flag. Stand up and fight for religious freedom!"

"America, God needs to hear from you not only in times of crisis. Why reject the One who has blessed you so much?"

"Chosen ignorance isn't ignorance. It's apathy. America, wake up and reclaim freedoms! Stop socialism and start patriotism!"

"America remains worth fighting for!"

"Veterans = Heroes"

"Veterans deserve the best -not the scraps! Support our veterans and vote for people who will do what's best for them!"

"Socialism has no place in America!"

"Let's get something straight: We Christians who oppose Obamacare dislike it because it allows government too much control of Christian ministries and their many outreaches (already muffled by regulations). Free us from socialism so that we can treat the poor with the richness of God's love in deed and truth!"

"I'd rather be bold about what's right than be silent and cry at what's left."

"I'd rather thank a veteran than seek out a celebrity. How about you?"

"There was a time when America didn't know of Ronald Reagan. God can rise up a good leader again. It's time to pray and work hard!"

"America, trust in God -not big government."

"Take note and vote! It's time for Christians to stand for what's right and not ignore the fight. We must spread love and peace while not allowing evil to gain ground."

"Hate policies, but not people. The Golden Rule still rules."

"Against all odds, this country formed by the grace of God. Against all odds, our country will soar again if she turns to the grace of God!"

"When people's hearts are changed by God, people's votes change for good. Pray for the USA."

"Be a good citizen! Forget about political ads as resources. Look into the facts for yourself. And register to vote. It's time for patriots to put their boots on the ground!"

"Apathetic people dismiss concerned citizens as alarmists. Hey, our Founding Fathers would relate to that. Be prayerful and careful to do the right thing before it's too late!"

"Some people put faith in silence and believe other people should stop sharing their faith. That's their belief. Why should their belief stop us from sharing ours? Yes, we're Christians. And we'll keep sharing God's love and truth. That's our belief."

"Don't give up hope! Hope in God, pray, and work hard. This country can soar again!"

"Not to vote is to admit defeat. Never give up! Pick the best available and then work to get the best next time!"

"Instead of obsessing over carbon footprints, it's time to give all unborn babies the freedom to leave footprints."

"This country needs more than a Ronald Reagan. America needs God."

"Don't fall asleep because you feel overwhelmed about our nation's needs. Keep moving forward in faith and for freedom! In God we trust!"

Appendix III: "America's Most Biblically-Hostile U.S. President" by David Barton

When one observes President Obama's unwillingness to accommodate America's four-century long religious conscience protection through his attempts to require Catholics to go against their own doctrines and beliefs, one is tempted to say that he is anti-Catholic. But that characterization would not be correct. Although he has recently singled out Catholics, he has equally targeted traditional Protestant beliefs over the past four years. So since he has attacked Catholics and Protestants, one is tempted to say that he is anti-Christian. But that, too, would be inaccurate. He has been equally disrespectful in his appalling treatment of religious Jews in general and Israel in particular. So perhaps the most accurate description of his antipathy toward Catholics, Protestants, religious Jews, and the Jewish nation would be to characterize him as anti-Biblical. And then when his hostility toward Biblical people of faith is contrasted with his preferential treatment of Muslims and Muslim nations, it further strengthens the accuracy of the anti-Biblical descriptor. In fact, there have been numerous clearly documented times when his pro-Islam positions have been the cause of his anti-Biblical actions.

Listed below in chronological order are (1) numerous records of his attacks on Biblical persons or organizations; (2) examples of the hostility toward Biblical faith that have become evident in the past three years in the Obama-led military; (3) a listing of his open attacks on Biblical values; and finally (4) a listing of numerous incidents of his preferential deference for Islam's activities and positions, including letting his Islamic advisors guide and influence his hostility toward people of Biblical faith.

1. Acts of hostility toward people of Biblical faith:
    *   April 2008 – Obama speaks disrespectfully of Christians, saying they "cling to guns or religion" and have an "antipathy to people who aren't like them." [1]
    *   February 2009 – Obama announces plans to revoke conscience protection for health workers who refuse to participate in medical activities that go against their beliefs, and fully implements the plan in February 2011. [2]
    *   April 2009 – When speaking at Georgetown University, Obama orders that a monogram symbolizing Jesus' name be covered when he is making his speech. [3]
    *   May 2009 – Obama declines to host services for the National Prayer Day (a day established by federal law) at the White House. [4]
    *   April 2009 – In a deliberate act of disrespect, Obama nominated three pro-abortion ambassadors to the Vatican; of course, the pro-life Vatican rejected all three. [5]
    *   October 19, 2010 – Obama begins deliberately omitting the phrase about "the Creator" when quoting the Declaration of Independence – an omission he has made on no less than seven occasions. [6]
    *   November 2010 – Obama misquotes the National Motto, saying it is "E pluribus unum" rather than "In God We Trust" as established by federal law. [7]
    *   January 2011 – After a federal law was passed to transfer a WWI Memorial in the Mojave Desert to private ownership, the U. S. Supreme Court ruled that the cross in the memorial

could continue to stand, but the Obama administration refused to allow the land to be transferred as required by law, and refused to allow the cross to be re-erected as ordered by the Court. [8]

- February 2011 – Although he filled posts in the State Department, for more than two years Obama did not fill the post of religious freedom ambassador, an official that works against religious persecution across the world; he filled it only after heavy pressure from the public and from Congress. [9]

- April 2011 – For the first time in American history, Obama urges passage of a non-discrimination law that does not contain hiring protections for religious groups, forcing religious organizations to hire according to federal mandates without regard to the dictates of their own faith, thus eliminating conscience protection in hiring. [10]

- August 2011 – The Obama administration releases its new health care rules that override religious conscience protections for medical workers in the areas of abortion and contraception. [11]

- November 2011 – President Obama opposes inclusion of President Franklin Roosevelt's famous D-Day Prayer in the WWII Memorial. [12]

- November 2011 – Unlike previous presidents, Obama studiously avoids any religious references in his Thanksgiving speech. [13]

- December 2011 – The Obama administration denigrates other countries' religious beliefs as an obstacle to radical homosexual rights. [14]

- January 2012 – The Obama administration argues that the First Amendment provides no protection for churches and synagogues in hiring their pastors and rabbis. [15]

- February 2012 – The Obama administration forgives student loans in exchange for public service, but announces it will no longer forgive student loans if the public service is related to religion. [16]

- January 2013 – Pastor Louie Giglio is pressured to remove himself from praying at the inauguration after it is discovered he once preached a sermon supporting the Biblical definition of marriage. [17]
- February 2013 – The Obama Administration announces that the rights of religious conscience for individuals will not be protected under the Affordable Care Act. [18]
- June 2013 – The Obama Department of Justice defunds a Young Marines chapter in Louisiana because their oath mentioned God, and another youth program because it permits a voluntary student-led prayer. [19]

2. Acts of hostility from the Obama-led military toward people of Biblical faith:
   - January 2010 – Because of "concerns" raised by the Department of Defense, tiny Bible verse references that had appeared for decades on scopes and gunsights were removed. [20]
   - June 2011 – The Department of Veterans Affairs forbids references to God and Jesus during burial ceremonies at Houston National Cemetery. [21]
   - August 2011 – The Air Force stops teaching the Just War theory to officers in California because the course is taught by chaplains and is based on a philosophy introduced by St. Augustine in the third century AD – a theory long taught by civilized nations across the world (except now, America). [22]
   - September 2011 – Air Force Chief of Staff prohibits commanders from notifying airmen of programs and services available to them from chaplains. [23]
   - September 2011 – The Army issues guidelines for Walter Reed Medical Center stipulating that "No religious items

(i.e. Bibles, reading materials and/or facts) are allowed to be given away or used during a visit." [24]

- November 2011 – The Air Force Academy rescinds support for Operation Christmas Child, a program to send holiday gifts to impoverished children across the world, because the program is run by a Christian charity. [25]
- November 2011 – Even while restricting and disapprobating Christian religious expressions, the Air Force Academy pays $80,000 to add a Stonehenge-like worship center for pagans, druids, witches and Wiccans at the Air Force Academy. [26]
- February 2012 – The U. S. Military Academy at West Point disinvites three star Army general and decorated war hero Lieutenant General William G. ("Jerry") Boykin (retired) from speaking at an event because he is an outspoken Christian. [27]
- February 2012 – The Air Force removes "God" from the patch of Rapid Capabilities Office (the word on the patch was in Latin: Dei). [28]
- February 2012 – The Army ordered Catholic chaplains not to read a letter to parishioners that their archbishop asked them to read. [29]
- April 2012 – A checklist for Air Force Inns will no longer include ensuring that a Bible is available in rooms for those who want to use them. [30]
- May 2012 – The Obama administration opposed legislation to protect the rights of conscience for military chaplains who do not wish to perform same-sex marriages in violation of their strongly-held religious beliefs. [31]
- June 2012 – Bibles for the American military have been printed in every conflict since the American Revolution, but the Obama Administration revokes the long-standing U. S. policy of allowing military service emblems to be placed on those military Bibles. [32]
- January 2013 – President Obama announced his opposition

to a provision in the 2013 National Defense Authorization Act protecting the rights of conscience for military chaplains. [33]

- April 2013 – Officials briefing U.S. Army soldiers placed "Evangelical Christianity" and "Catholicism" in a list that also included Al-Qaeda, Muslim Brotherhood, and Hamas as examples of "religious extremism." [34]

- April 2013 – The U.S. Army directs troops to scratch off and paint over tiny Scripture verse references that for decades had been forged into weapon scopes. [35]

- April 2013 - The Air Force creates a "religious tolerance" policy but consults only a militant atheist group to do so — a group whose leader has described military personnel who are religious as 'spiritual rapists' and 'human monsters' [36] and who also says that soldiers who proselytize are guilty of treason and sedition and should be punished to hold back a "tidal wave of fundamentalists." [37]

- May 2013 - The Pentagon announces that "Air Force members are free to express their personal religious beliefs as long as it does not make others uncomfortable. "Proselytizing (inducing someone to convert to one's faith) goes over that line," [38] affirming if a sharing of faith makes someone feel uncomfortable that it could be a court-marital offense [39] — the military equivalent of a civil felony.

- May 2013 - An Air Force officer was actually made to remove a personal Bible from his own desk because it "might" appear that he was condoning the particular religion to which he belonged. [40]

- June 2013 - The U. S. Air Force, in consultation with the Pentagon, removed an inspirational painting that for years has been hanging at Mountain Home Air Force Base because its title was "Blessed Are The Peacemakers" — a phrase from Matthew 5:9 in the Bible. [41]

- June 2013 – The Obama administration "strongly objects" to a Defense Authorization amendment to protect the constitutionally-guaranteed religious rights of soldiers and chaplains, claiming that it would have an "adverse effect on good order, discipline, morale, and mission accomplishment." [42]

- July 2013 - When an Air Force sergeant with years of military service questioned a same-sex marriage ceremony performed at the Air Force Academy's chapel, he received a letter of reprimand telling him that if he disagreed, he needed to get out of the military. His current six-year reenlistment was then reduced to only one-year, with the notification that he "be prepared to retire at the end of this year." [43]
- July 2013 - An Air Force chaplain who posted a website article on the importance of faith and the origin of the phrase "There are no atheists in foxholes" was officially ordered to remove his post because some were offended by the use of that famous World War II phrase. [44]

3. Acts of hostility toward Biblical values:
   - January 2009 – Obama lifts restrictions on U.S. government funding for groups that provide abortion services or counseling abroad, forcing taxpayers to fund pro-abortion groups that either promote or perform abortions in other nations. [45]
   - January 2009 – President Obama's nominee for deputy secretary of state asserts that American taxpayers are required to pay for abortions and that limits on abortion funding are unconstitutional. [46]
   - March 2009 – The Obama administration shut out pro-life groups from attending a White House-sponsored health care summit. [47]
   - March 2009 – Obama orders taxpayer funding of embryonic stem cell research. [48]
   - March 2009 – Obama gave $50 million for the UNFPA, the UN population agency that promotes abortion and works

closely with Chinese population control officials who use forced abortions and involuntary sterilizations. [49]

- May 2009 – The White House budget eliminates all funding for abstinence-only education and replaces it with "comprehensive" sexual education, repeatedly proven to increase teen pregnancies and abortions. [50] He continues the deletion in subsequent budgets. [51]

- May 2009 – Obama officials assemble a terrorism dictionary calling pro-life advocates violent and charging that they use racism in their "criminal" activities. [52]

- July 2009 – The Obama administration illegally extends federal benefits to same-sex partners of Foreign Service and Executive Branch employees, in direction violation of the federal Defense of Marriage Act. [53]

- September 16, 2009 – The Obama administration appoints as EEOC Commissioner Chai Feldblum, who asserts that society should "not tolerate" any "private beliefs," including religious beliefs, if they may negatively affect homosexual "equality." [54]

- July 2010 – The Obama administration uses federal funds in violation of federal law to get Kenya to change its constitution to include abortion. [55]

- August 2010 – The Obama administration Cuts funding for 176 abstinence education programs. [56]

- September 2010 – The Obama administration tells researchers to ignore a judge's decision striking down federal funding for embryonic stem cell research. [57]

- February 2011 – Obama directs the Justice Department to stop defending the federal Defense of Marriage Act. [58]

- March 2011 – The Obama administration refuses to investigate videos showing Planned Parenthood helping alleged sex traffickers get abortions for victimized underage girls. [59]

- July 2011 – Obama allows homosexuals to serve openly in the military, reversing a policy originally instituted by George Washington in March 1778. [60]

- September 2011 – The Pentagon directs that military chaplains may perform same-sex marriages at military facilities in violation of the federal Defense of Marriage Act. [61]
- October 2011 – The Obama administration eliminates federal grants to the U.S. Conference of Catholic Bishops for their extensive programs that aid victims of human trafficking because the Catholic Church is anti-abortion. [62]
- July 2012 - The Pentagon, for the first time, allows service members to wear their uniforms while marching in a parade - specifically, a gay pride parade in San Diego. [63]
- December 2012 – Despite having campaigned to recognize Jerusalem as Israel's capital, President Obama once again suspends the provisions of the Jerusalem Embassy Act of 1995 which requires the United States to recognize Jerusalem as the capital of Israel and to move the American Embassy there. [64]
- April 2013 – The United States Agency for Internal Development (USAID), an official foreign policy agency of the U.S. government, begins a program to train homosexual activists in various countries around the world to overturn traditional marriage and anti-sodomy laws, targeting first those countries with strong Catholic influences, including Ecuador, Honduras, and Guatemala. [65]
- June 2013 – The Obama Administration finalizes requirements that under the Obamacare insurance program, employers must make available abortion-causing drugs, regardless of the religious conscience objections of many employers and even despite the directive of several federal courts to protect the religious conscience of employers. [66]
- August 2013 - Non-profit charitable hospitals, especially faith-based ones, will face large fines or lose their tax-exempt

status if they don't comply with new strangling paperwork requirements related to giving free treatment to poor clients who do not have Obamacare insurance coverage. [67] Ironically, the first hospital in America was founded as a charitable institution in 1751 by Benjamin Franklin, and its logo was the Good Samaritan, with Luke 10:35 inscribed below him: "Take care of him, and I will repay thee," being designed specifically to offer free medical care to the poor. [68] Benjamin Franklin's hospital would likely be fined unless he placed more resources and funds into paperwork rather than helping the poor under the new faith-hostile policy of the Obama administration.

- August 2013 - USAID, a federal government agency, shut down a conference in South Korea the night before it was scheduled to take place because some of the presentations were not pro-abortion but instead presented information on abortion complications, including the problems of "preterm births, mental health issues, and maternal mortality" among women giving birth who had previous abortions. [69]

4. Acts of preferentialism for Islam:
   - May 2009 – While Obama does not host any National Day of Prayer event at the White House, he does host White House Iftar dinners in honor of Ramadan. [70]
   - April 2010 – Christian leader Franklin Graham is disinvited from the Pentagon's National Day of Prayer Event because of complaints from the Muslim community. [71]
   - April 2010 – The Obama administration requires rewriting of government documents and a change in administration vocabulary to remove terms that are deemed offensive to Muslims, including jihad, jihadists, terrorists, radical Islamic, etc. [72]
   - August 2010 – Obama speaks with great praise of Islam and condescendingly of Christianity. [73]

- August 2010 – Obama went to great lengths to speak out on multiple occasions on behalf of building an Islamic mosque at Ground Zero, while at the same time he was silent about a Christian church being denied permission to rebuild at that location. [74]
- 2010 – While every White House traditionally issues hundreds of official proclamations and statements on numerous occasions, this White House avoids traditional Biblical holidays and events but regularly recognizes major Muslim holidays, as evidenced by its 2010 statements on Ramadan, Eid-ul-Fitr, Hajj, and Eid-ul-Adha. [75]
- October 2011 – Obama's Muslim advisers block Middle Eastern Christians' access to the White House. [76]
- February 2012 – The Obama administration makes effulgent apologies for Korans being burned by the U. S. military, [77] but when Bibles were burned by the military, numerous reasons were offered why it was the right thing to do. [78]

Many of these actions are literally unprecedented – this is the first time they have happened in four centuries of American history. The hostility of President Obama toward Biblical faith and values is without equal from any previous American president.

[1] Sarah Pulliam Baily, "Obama: 'They cling to guns or religion'," *Christianity Today*, April 13, 2008.

[2] Aliza Marcus, "Obama to Lift 'Conscience' Rule for Health Workers," *Bloomberg*, February 27, 2009; Sarah Pulliam Baily, "Obama Admin. Changes Bush 'Conscience' Rule for Health Workers," *Christianity Today*, February 18, 2011.

[3] Jim Lovino, "Jesus Missing From Obama's Georgetown Speech," *NBC Washington*, April 17, 2009.

[4] Johanna Neuman, "Obama end Bush-era National Prayer Day Service at White House," *Los Angeles Times*, May 7, 2009.

[5] Chris McGreal, "Vatican vetoes Barack Obama's nominees for U.S. Ambassador," *The Guardian*, April 14, 2009.

[6] Meredith Jessup, "Obama Continues to Omit 'Creator' From Declaration of Independence," *The Blaze*, October 19, 2010.

[7] "Remarks by the President at the University of Indonesia in Jakarta, Indonesia," *The White House*, November 10, 2010.

[8] LadyImpactOhio, "Feds sued by Veterans to allow stolen Mojave Desert Cross to be rebuilt," *Red State*, January 14, 2011.

[9] Marrianne Medlin, "Amid criticism, President Obama moves to fill vacant religious ambassador post," *Catholic News Agency*, February 9, 2011; Thomas F. Farr, "Undefender of the Faith," *Foreign Policy*, April 5, 2012.

[10] Chris Johnson, "ENDA passage effort renewed with Senate introduction," *Washington Blade*, April 15, 2011.

[11] Chuck Donovan, "HHS's New Health Guidelines Trample on Conscience," *Heritage Foundation*, August 2, 2011.

[12] Todd Starns, "Obama Administration Opposes FDR Prayer at WWII Memorial," *Fox News*, November 4, 2011.

[13] Joel Siegel, "Obama Omits God From Thanksgiving Speech, Riles Critics," *ABC News*, November 25, 2011.

[14] Hillary Rodham Clinton, "Remarks in Recognition of International Human Rights Day," *U.S. Department of State*, December 6, 2011.

[15] Ted Olson, "Church Wins Firing Case at Supreme Court," *Christianity Today*, January 11, 2012.

[16] Audrey Hudson, "Obama administration religious service for student loan forgiveness," *Human Events*, February 15, 2012.

[17] Sheryl Gay Stolberg, "Minister Backs Out of Speech at Inaugural," *New York Times*, January 10, 2013; Eric Marrapodi, "Giglio bows out of inauguration over sermon on gays," *CNN*, January 10, 2013.

[18] Steven Ertelt, "Obama Admin's HHS Mandate Revision Likely Excludes Hobby Lobby," *LifeNews.com*, February 1, 2013; Dan Merica, "Obama proposal would let religious groups opt-out of contraception mandate," *CNN*, February 1, 2013.

[19] Todd Starnes, "DOJ Defunds At-Risk Youth Programs over "God" Reference," *Townhall*, June 25, 2013.

[20] Todd Spangler, "U.S. firm to remove Bible references from gun sights," *USA Today*, January 21, 2010.

[21] "Houston Veterans Claim Censorship of Prayers, Including Ban of 'God' and 'Jesus'," *Fox News*, June 29, 2011.

[22] Jason Ukman, "Air Force suspends ethics course that used Bible passages that train missle launch officers," *Washington Post*, August 2, 2011.

[23] "Maintaining Government Neutrality Regarding Religion," *Department of the Air Force*, September 1, 2011.

[24] "Wounded, Ill, and Injured Partners in Care Guidelines," *Department of the Navy* (accessed on February 29, 2012).

[25] "Air Force Academy Backs Away from Christmas Charity," *Fox News Radio*, November 4, 2011.

[26] Jenny Dean, "Air Force Academy adapts to pagans, druids, witches and Wiccans," *Los Angeles Times*, November 26, 2011.

[27] Ken Blackwell, "Gen. Boykin Blocked At West Point," *cnsnews. com*, February 1, 2012.

[28] Geoff Herbert, " Air Force unit removes 'God' from logo; lawmakers warn of 'dangerous precedent'," *syracuse.com*, February 9, 2012.

[29] Todd Starnes, "Army Silences Catholic Chaplains," *Fox News Radio*, February 6, 2012.

[30] Markeshia Ricks, "Bible checklist for Air Force lodges going away," *Air Force Times*, April 16, 2012.

[31] Patrick Goodenough, "White House 'Strongly Objects' to Legislation Protecting Military Chaplains from Doing Same-Sex Weddings or Being Forced to Act Against Conscience," *cnsnews.com*, May 16, 2012.

[32] "U.S. military insignia no longer allowed on Bibles," *CBN News*, June 14, 2012.

[33] Billy Hallowell, "Obama Opposes NDAA's 'Rights of Conscience' for Military Chaplains & Members, Vows to Protects Rights of Gays," *The Blaze*, January 4, 2013; Paul Conner, "Obama calls NDAA conscience clause for military chaplains 'unnecessary and ill-advised'," *The Daily Caller*, January 3, 2013.

[34] Jack Minor, "Military Warned 'evangelicals' No. 1 Threat," *WND*, April 5, 2013.

[35] Todd Starnes, "Army Removes Bible Reference from Scopes," *Fox News Radio*, April 22, 2013.

[36] "Chaplain endorsers ask Air Force for equal time," *Alliance Defending Freedom*, April 30, 2013.

[37] Todd Starnes, "Pentagon: Religious Proselytizing is Not Permitted," *Fox News Radio*, April 30, 2013.

[38] "Liberty Institute Calls On U.S. Department Of Defense To Abandon Shift In Military's Proselytizing Policy," *PR Newswire*, May 7, 2013; Todd Starnes, "Air Force Officer Told to Remove Bible from Desk," *Townhall.com*, May 3, 2013.

[39] "Pentagon May Court Martial Soldiers Who Share Christian Faith," *Breitbart*, May 1, 2013.

[40] Todd Starnes, "Air Force Officer Told to Remove Bible from Desk," *Townhall.com*, May 3, 2013.

[41] Hellen Cook, "Pentagon Censors Christian Art," *Christian News Wire*, January 21, 2010.

[42] Todd Starnes, "Obama 'Strongly Objects' to Religious Liberty Amendment," *Townhall*, June 12, 2013.

[43] Chad Groening, "Attorney demands answers for Air National Guard sergeant punished for beliefs," *OneNewsNow*, July 15, 2013.

[44] Todd Starnes, "Chaplain Ordered to Remove Religious Essay From Military Website," *FoxNews Radio*, July 24, 2013.

[45] Jeff Mason and Deborah Charles, "Obama lifts restrictions on abortion funding," *Reuters*, January 23, 2009.

[46] "Obama pick: Taxpayers must fund abortions," *World Net Daily*, January 27, 2009.

[47] Steven Ertelt, "Pro-Life Groups Left Off Obama's Health Care Summit List, Abortion Advocates OK," *LifeNews*, March 5, 2009.

[48] "Obama Signs Order Lifting Restrictions on Stem Cell Research Funding," *Fox News*, March 9, 2009.

[49] Steven Ertelt, "Obama Administration Announces $50 Million for Pro-Forced Abortion UNFPA," *LifeNews*, March 26, 2009; Steven

Ertelt, "President Barack Obama's Pro-Abortion Record: A Pro-Life Compilation," *LifeNews*, February 11, 2012.

[50] Steven Ertelt, "Barack Obama's Federal Budget Eliminates Funding for Abstinence-Only Education," *LifeNews*, May 8, 2009.

[51] Steven Ertelt, "Obama Budget Funds Sex Ed Over Abstinence on 16-1 Margin," *LifeNews*, February 14, 2011.

[52] Steven Ertelt, "Obama Admin Terrorism Dictionary Calls Pro-Life Advocates Violent, Racist," *LifeNews*, May 5, 2009.

[53] "Memorandum for the Heads of Executive Departments and Agencies," *The White House*, June 17, 2009.

[54] Matt Cover, "Obama's EEOC Nominee: Society Should 'Not Tolerate Private Beliefs' That 'Adversely Affect' Homosexuals," *cnsnews.com*, January 18, 2010.

[55] Tess Civantos, "White House Spent $23M of Taxpayer Money to Back Kenyan Constitution That Legalizes Abortion, GOP Reps Say," *Fox News*, July 22, 2010.

[56] Steven Ertelt, "Obama, Congress Cut Funding for 176 Abstinence Programs Despite New Study," *LifeNews*, August 26, 2010.

[57] Steven Ertelt, "President Barack Obama's Pro-Abortion Record: A Pro-Life Compilation," *LifeNews*, February 11, 2012.

[58] Brian Montopoli, "Obama administration will no longer defend DOMA," *CBSNews*, February 23, 2011.

[59] Steven Ertelt, "Obama Admin Ignores Planned Parenthood Sex Trafficking Videos," *LifeNews*, March 2, 2011.

[60] Elisabeth Bumiller, "Obama Ends 'Don't Ask, Don't Tell' Policy," *New York Times*, July 22, 2011; George Washington, The Writings of George Washington, John C. Fitzpatrick, editor (Washington: U. S.

Government Printing Office, 1934), Vol. XI, pp. 83-84, from General Orders at Valley Forge on March 14, 1778.

[61] Luis Martinez, "Will Same Sex Marriages Pose a Dilemma for Military Chaplains?," *ABC News*, October 12, 2011.

[62] Jerry Markon, "Health, abortion issues split Obama administration and Catholic groups," *Washington Post*, October 31, 2011.

[63] "Pentagon: Service members now allowed to wear uniforms in gay pride parades," *NY Daily News*, July 19, 2012.

[64] Ken Blackwell, "Guest Opinion: Take a Risk for Peace. Move our Embassy to Jerusalem!," *Catholic Online*, June 5, 2013.

[65] Tony Perkins, "Obama administration begins training homosexual activists around the world," *LifeSiteNews*, June 6, 2013.

[66] "Obama Administration Ignores Outcries, Finalizes HHS Mandate Targeting Religious Freedom," *Liberty Counsel*, July 1, 2013; Baptist Press, "Moore, others: Final mandate rules fail," *Townhall*, July 1, 2013.

[67] Patrick Howley, "Obamacare installs new scrutiny, fines for charitable hospitals that treat uninsured people," *The Daily Caller*, August 8, 2013.

[68] "The Story of the Creation of the Nation's First Hospital," *University of Pennsylvania Health System* (accessed August 14, 2013).

[69] Wendy Wright," USAID Rep Shuts Down Workshop on Abortion Complications," *Catholic Family & Human Rights Institute*, August 9, 2013.

[70] Barack Obama, " Remarks by the President at Iftar Dinner," *The White House*, September 1, 2009; Kristi Keck, " Obama tones down National Day of Prayer observance," *CNN*, May 6, 2009; Dan Gilgoff,

" The White House on National Day of Prayer: A Proclamation, but No Formal Ceremony," *U.S. News*, May 1, 2009.

[71] "Franklin Graham Regrets Army's Decision to Rescind Invite to Pentagon Prayer Service," *Fox News*, April 22, 2010.

[72] "Obama Bans Islam, Jihad From National Security Strategy Document," *Fox News*, April 7, 2010; "Counterterror Adviser Defends Jihad as 'Legitimate Tenet of Islam'," *Fox News*, May 27, 2010; "'Islamic Radicalism' Nixed From Obama Document," *CBSNews*, April 7, 2010.

[73] Chuck Norris, " President Obama: Muslim Missionary? (Part 2)," *Townhall.com*, August 24, 2010; Chuck Norris, "President Obama: Muslim Missionary?," *Townhall.com*, August 17, 2010.

[74] Barack Obama, "Remarks by the President at Iftar Dinner," *The White House*, August 13, 2010; "Obama Comes Out in Favor of Allowing Mosque Near Ground Zero," *Fox News*, August 13, 2010; Pamela Geller, "Islamic Supremacism Trumps Christianity at Ground Zero," *American Thinker*, July 21, 2011.

[75] "WH Fails to Release Easter Proclamation," *Fox Nation*, April 25, 2011; "President Obama ignores most holy Christian holiday; AFA calls act intentional," *American Family Association* (accessed on February 29, 2012).

[76] "Report: Obama's Muslim Advisers Block Middle Eastern Christians' Access to the White House," *Big Peace* (accessed on February 29, 2012).

[77] Masoud Popalzai and Nick Paton Walsh, " Obama apologizes to Afghanistan for Quran burning," *CNN*, February 23, 2012.

[78] "Military burns unsolicited Bibles sent to Afghanistan," *CNN*, May 22, 2009.

"Must-Read" Founding Documents: The Transcription of the Original Declaration of Independence

IN CONGRESS, July 4, 1776.

The unanimous Declaration of the thirteen united States of America,

When in the Course of human events, it becomes necessary for one people to dissolve the political bands which have connected them with another, and to assume among the powers of the earth, the separate and equal station to which the Laws of Nature and of Nature's God entitle them, a decent respect to the opinions of mankind requires that they should declare the causes which impel them to the separation.

We hold these truths to be self-evident, that all men are created equal, that they are endowed by their Creator with certain unalienable Rights, that among these are Life, Liberty and the pursuit of Happiness.--That to secure these rights, Governments are instituted among Men, deriving their just powers from the consent of the governed, --That whenever any Form of Government becomes destructive of these ends, it is the Right of the People to alter or to abolish it, and to institute new Government, laying its foundation on such principles and organizing its powers in such form, as to them shall seem most likely to affect their Safety and Happiness. Prudence, indeed, will dictate that Governments long established should not be changed for light and transient causes; and accordingly all experience hath shewn, that mankind are more disposed to suffer, while evils are sufferable, than to right themselves by abolishing the forms to which they are accustomed. But when a long train of abuses and usurpations, pursuing invariably the same Object evinces a design to reduce them under absolute Despotism, it is their right, it is their duty, to throw off such Government, and to provide new Guards for their future security.--Such has been the patient sufferance of these Colonies; and such is now the necessity which constrains them to alter their former Systems of Government. The history of the present King of Great Britain is a history of repeated injuries and usurpations, all having in direct object the establishment of an absolute Tyranny over these States. To prove this, let Facts be submitted to a candid world.

He has refused his Assent to Laws, the most wholesome and necessary for the public good.

He has forbidden his Governors to pass Laws of immediate and pressing importance, unless suspended in their operation till his Assent should be obtained; and when so suspended, he has utterly neglected to attend to them.

He has refused to pass other Laws for the accommodation of large districts of people, unless those people would relinquish the right of Representation in the Legislature, a right inestimable to them and formidable to tyrants only.

He has called together legislative bodies at places unusual, uncomfortable, and distant from the depository of their public Records, for the sole purpose of fatiguing them into compliance with his measures.

He has dissolved Representative Houses repeatedly, for opposing with manly firmness his invasions on the rights of the people.

He has refused for a long time, after such dissolutions, to cause others to be elected; whereby the Legislative powers, incapable of Annihilation, have returned to the People at large for their exercise;

the State remaining in the mean time exposed to all the dangers of invasion from without, and convulsions within.

He has endeavoured to prevent the population of these States; for that purpose obstructing the Laws for Naturalization of Foreigners; refusing to pass others to encourage their migrations hither, and raising the conditions of new Appropriations of Lands.

He has obstructed the Administration of Justice, by refusing his Assent to Laws for establishing Judiciary powers.

He has made Judges dependent on his Will alone, for the tenure of their offices, and the amount and payment of their salaries.

He has erected a multitude of New Offices, and sent hither swarms of Officers to harrass our people, and eat out their substance.

He has kept among us, in times of peace, Standing Armies without the Consent of our legislatures.

He has affected to render the Military independent of and superior to the Civil power.

He has combined with others to subject us to a jurisdiction foreign to our constitution, and unacknowledged by our laws; giving his Assent to their Acts of pretended Legislation:

For Quartering large bodies of armed troops among us:

For protecting them, by a mock Trial, from punishment for any Murders which they should commit on the Inhabitants of these States:

For cutting off our Trade with all parts of the world:

For imposing Taxes on us without our Consent:

For depriving us in many cases, of the benefits of Trial by Jury:

For transporting us beyond Seas to be tried for pretended offences

For abolishing the free System of English Laws in a neighbouring Province, establishing therein an Arbitrary government, and enlarging its Boundaries so as to render it at once an example and fit instrument for introducing the same absolute rule into these Colonies:

For taking away our Charters, abolishing our most valuable Laws, and altering fundamentally the Forms of our Governments:

For suspending our own Legislatures, and declaring themselves invested with power to legislate for us in all cases whatsoever.

He has abdicated Government here, by declaring us out of his Protection and waging War against us.

He has plundered our seas, ravaged our Coasts, burnt our towns, and destroyed the lives of our people.

He is at this time transporting large Armies of foreign Mercenaries to compleat the works of death, desolation and tyranny, already begun with circumstances of Cruelty & perfidy scarcely paralleled in the most barbarous ages, and totally unworthy the Head of a civilized nation.

He has constrained our fellow Citizens taken Captive on the high Seas to bear Arms against their Country, to become the executioners of their friends and Brethren, or to fall themselves by their Hands.

He has excited domestic insurrections amongst us, and has endeavoured to bring on the inhabitants of our frontiers, the merciless Indian Savages, whose known rule of warfare, is an undistinguished destruction of all ages, sexes and conditions.

In every stage of these Oppressions We have Petitioned for Redress in the most humble terms: Our repeated Petitions have been answered only by repeated injury. A Prince whose character is thus marked by every act which may define a Tyrant, is unfit to be the ruler of a free people.

Nor have We been wanting in attentions to our Brittish brethren. We have warned them from time to time of attempts by their legislature to extend an unwarrantable jurisdiction over us. We have reminded them of the circumstances of our emigration and settlement here. We have appealed to their native justice and magnanimity, and we have conjured them by the ties of our common kindred to disavow these usurpations, which, would inevitably interrupt our connections and correspondence. They too have been deaf to the voice of justice and of consanguinity. We must, therefore, acquiesce in the necessity, which denounces our Separation, and hold them, as we hold the rest of mankind, Enemies in War, in Peace Friends.

We, therefore, the Representatives of the united States of America, in General Congress, Assembled, appealing to the Supreme Judge of the world for the rectitude of our intentions, do, in the Name, and by Authority of the good People of these Colonies, solemnly publish and declare, That these United Colonies are, and of Right ought to be Free and Independent States; that they are Absolved from all Allegiance to the British Crown, and that all political connection between them and the State of Great Britain, is and ought to be totally dissolved; and that as Free and Independent States, they have full Power to levy War, conclude Peace, contract Alliances, establish Commerce, and to do all other Acts and Things which Independent States may of right do. And for the support of this Declaration, with a firm reliance on the protection of divine Providence, we mutually pledge to each other our Lives, our Fortunes and our sacred Honor.

The 56 signatures on the Declaration appear in the positions indicated:
Column 1
Georgia:
Button Gwinnett
Lyman Hall
George Walton
Column 2
North Carolina:
William Hooper
Joseph Hewes
John Penn
South Carolina:
Edward Rutledge
Thomas Heyward, Jr.
Thomas Lynch, Jr.
Arthur Middleton
Column 3
Massachusetts:
John Hancock
Maryland:
Samuel Chase

William Paca
Thomas Stone
Charles Carroll of Carrollton
Virginia:
George Wythe
Richard Henry Lee
Thomas Jefferson
Benjamin Harrison
Thomas Nelson, Jr.
Francis Lightfoot Lee
Carter Braxton
Column 4
Pennsylvania:
Robert Morris
Benjamin Rush
Benjamin Franklin
John Morton
George Clymer
James Smith
George Taylor
James Wilson
George Ross
Delaware:
Caesar Rodney
George Read
Thomas McKean
Column 5
New York:
William Floyd
Philip Livingston
Francis Lewis
Lewis Morris
New Jersey:
Richard Stockton

John Witherspoon
Francis Hopkinson
John Hart
Abraham Clark
Column 6
New Hampshire:
Josiah Bartlett
William Whipple
Massachusetts:
Samuel Adams
John Adams
Robert Treat Paine
Elbridge Gerry
Rhode Island:
Stephen Hopkins
William Ellery
Connecticut:
Roger Sherman
Samuel Huntington
William Williams
Oliver Wolcott
New Hampshire:
Matthew Thornton

The Transcription of the Original Constitution of the United States of America

Preamble

We the People of the United States, in Order to form a more perfect Union, establish Justice, insure domestic Tranquility, provide for the common defence, promote the general Welfare, and secure the Blessings of Liberty to ourselves and our Posterity, do ordain and establish this Constitution for the United States of America.

Article. I.

Section. 1.

All legislative Powers herein granted shall be vested in a Congress of the United States, which shall consist of a Senate and House of Representatives.

Section. 2.

The House of Representatives shall be composed of Members chosen every second Year by the People of the several States, and the Electors in each State shall have the Qualifications requisite for Electors of the most numerous Branch of the State Legislature.

No Person shall be a Representative who shall not have attained to the Age of twenty five Years, and been seven Years a Citizen of the

United States, and who shall not, when elected, be an Inhabitant of that State in which he shall be chosen.

Representatives and direct Taxes shall be apportioned among the several States which may be included within this Union, according to their respective Numbers, which shall be determined by adding to the whole Number of free Persons, including those bound to Service for a Term of Years, and excluding Indians not taxed, three fifths of all other Persons. The actual Enumeration shall be made within three Years after the first Meeting of the Congress of the United States, and within every subsequent Term of ten Years, in such Manner as they shall by Law direct. The Number of Representatives shall not exceed one for every thirty Thousand, but each State shall have at Least one Representative; and until such enumeration shall be made, the State of New Hampshire shall be entitled to chuse three, Massachusetts eight, Rhode-Island and Providence Plantations one, Connecticut five, New-York six, New Jersey four, Pennsylvania eight, Delaware one, Maryland six, Virginia ten, North Carolina five, South Carolina five, and Georgia three.

When vacancies happen in the Representation from any State, the Executive Authority thereof shall issue Writs of Election to fill such Vacancies.

The House of Representatives shall chuse their Speaker and other Officers; and shall have the sole Power of Impeachment.

Section. 3.

The Senate of the United States shall be composed of two Senators from each State, chosen by the Legislature thereof for six Years; and each Senator shall have one Vote.

Immediately after they shall be assembled in Consequence of the first Election, they shall be divided as equally as may be into three Classes. The Seats of the Senators of the first Class shall be vacated at the Expiration of the second Year, of the second Class at the Expiration of the fourth Year, and of the third Class at the Expiration of the sixth Year, so that one third may be chosen every second Year;

and if Vacancies happen by Resignation, or otherwise, during the Recess of the Legislature of any State, the Executive thereof may make temporary Appointments until the next Meeting of the Legislature, which shall then fill such Vacancies.

No Person shall be a Senator who shall not have attained to the Age of thirty Years, and been nine Years a Citizen of the United States, and who shall not, when elected, be an Inhabitant of that State for which he shall be chosen.

The Vice President of the United States shall be President of the Senate, but shall have no Vote, unless they be equally divided.

The Senate shall chuse their other Officers, and also a President pro tempore, in the Absence of the Vice President, or when he shall exercise the Office of President of the United States.

The Senate shall have the sole Power to try all Impeachments. When sitting for that Purpose, they shall be on Oath or Affirmation. When the President of the United States is tried, the Chief Justice shall preside: And no Person shall be convicted without the Concurrence of two thirds of the Members present.

Judgment in Cases of Impeachment shall not extend further than to removal from Office, and disqualification to hold and enjoy any Office of honor, Trust or Profit under the United States: but the Party convicted shall nevertheless be liable and subject to Indictment, Trial, Judgment and Punishment, according to Law.

Section. 4.

The Times, Places and Manner of holding Elections for Senators and Representatives, shall be prescribed in each State by the Legislature thereof; but the Congress may at any time by Law make or alter such Regulations, except as to the Places of chusing Senators.

The Congress shall assemble at least once in every Year, and such Meeting shall be on the first Monday in December, unless they shall by Law appoint a different Day.

Section. 5.

Each House shall be the Judge of the Elections, Returns and Qualifications of its own Members, and a Majority of each shall constitute a Quorum to do Business; but a smaller Number may adjourn from day to day, and may be authorized to compel the Attendance of absent Members, in such Manner, and under such Penalties as each House may provide.

Each House may determine the Rules of its Proceedings, punish its Members for disorderly Behaviour, and, with the Concurrence of two thirds, expel a Member.

Each House shall keep a Journal of its Proceedings, and from time to time publish the same, excepting such Parts as may in their Judgment require Secrecy; and the Yeas and Nays of the Members of either House on any question shall, at the Desire of one fifth of those Present, be entered on the Journal.

Neither House, during the Session of Congress, shall, without the Consent of the other, adjourn for more than three days, nor to any other Place than that in which the two Houses shall be sitting.

Section. 6.

The Senators and Representatives shall receive a Compensation for their Services, to be ascertained by Law, and paid out of the Treasury of the United States. They shall in all Cases, except Treason, Felony and Breach of the Peace, be privileged from Arrest during their Attendance at the Session of their respective Houses, and in going to and returning from the same; and for any Speech or Debate in either House, they shall not be questioned in any other Place.

No Senator or Representative shall, during the Time for which he was elected, be appointed to any civil Office under the Authority of the United States, which shall have been created, or the Emoluments whereof shall have been encreased during such time; and no Person holding any Office under the United States, shall be a Member of either House during his Continuance in Office.

Section. 7.

All Bills for raising Revenue shall originate in the House of Representatives; but the Senate may propose or concur with Amendments as on other Bills.

Every Bill which shall have passed the House of Representatives and the Senate, shall, before it become a Law, be presented to the President of the United States: If he approve he shall sign it, but if not he shall return it, with his Objections to that House in which it shall have originated, who shall enter the Objections at large on their Journal, and proceed to reconsider it. If after such Reconsideration two thirds of that House shall agree to pass the Bill, it shall be sent, together with the Objections, to the other House, by which it shall likewise be reconsidered, and if approved by two thirds of that House, it shall become a Law. But in all such Cases the Votes of both Houses shall be determined by yeas and Nays, and the Names of the Persons voting for and against the Bill shall be entered on the Journal of each House respectively. If any Bill shall not be returned by the President within ten Days (Sundays excepted) after it shall have been presented to him, the Same shall be a Law, in like Manner as if he had signed it, unless the Congress by their Adjournment prevent its Return, in which Case it shall not be a Law.

Every Order, Resolution, or Vote to which the Concurrence of the Senate and House of Representatives may be necessary (except on a question of Adjournment) shall be presented to the President of the United States; and before the Same shall take Effect, shall be approved by him, or being disapproved by him, shall be repassed by two thirds of the Senate and House of Representatives, according to the Rules and Limitations prescribed in the Case of a Bill.

Section. 8.

The Congress shall have Power To lay and collect Taxes, Duties, Imposts and Excises, to pay the Debts and provide for the common Defence and general Welfare of the United States; but all Duties, Imposts and Excises shall be uniform throughout the United States;

To borrow Money on the credit of the United States;

To regulate Commerce with foreign Nations, and among the several States, and with the Indian Tribes;

To establish an uniform Rule of Naturalization, and uniform Laws on the subject of Bankruptcies throughout the United States;

To coin Money, regulate the Value thereof, and of foreign Coin, and fix the Standard of Weights and Measures;

To provide for the Punishment of counterfeiting the Securities and current Coin of the United States;

To establish Post Offices and post Roads;

To promote the Progress of Science and useful Arts, by securing for limited Times to Authors and Inventors the exclusive Right to their respective Writings and Discoveries;

To constitute Tribunals inferior to the supreme Court;

To define and punish Piracies and Felonies committed on the high Seas, and Offences against the Law of Nations;

To declare War, grant Letters of Marque and Reprisal, and make Rules concerning Captures on Land and Water;

To raise and support Armies, but no Appropriation of Money to that Use shall be for a longer Term than two Years;

To provide and maintain a Navy;

To make Rules for the Government and Regulation of the land and naval Forces;

To provide for calling forth the Militia to execute the Laws of the Union, suppress Insurrections and repel Invasions;

To provide for organizing, arming, and disciplining, the Militia, and for governing such Part of them as may be employed in the Service of the United States, reserving to the States respectively, the Appointment of the Officers, and the Authority of training the Militia according to the discipline prescribed by Congress;

To exercise exclusive Legislation in all Cases whatsoever, over such District (not exceeding ten Miles square) as may, by Cession of particular States, and the Acceptance of Congress, become the Seat of the Government of the United States, and to exercise like Authority over all Places purchased by the Consent of the Legislature of the

State in which the Same shall be, for the Erection of Forts, Magazines, Arsenals, dock-Yards, and other needful Buildings;--And

To make all Laws which shall be necessary and proper for carrying into Execution the foregoing Powers, and all other Powers vested by this Constitution in the Government of the United States, or in any Department or Officer thereof.

Section. 9.

The Migration or Importation of such Persons as any of the States now existing shall think proper to admit, shall not be prohibited by the Congress prior to the Year one thousand eight hundred and eight, but a Tax or duty may be imposed on such Importation, not exceeding ten dollars for each Person.

The Privilege of the Writ of Habeas Corpus shall not be suspended, unless when in Cases of Rebellion or Invasion the public Safety may require it.

No Bill of Attainder or ex post facto Law shall be passed.

No Capitation, or other direct, Tax shall be laid, unless in Proportion to the Census or enumeration herein before directed to be taken.

No Tax or Duty shall be laid on Articles exported from any State.

No Preference shall be given by any Regulation of Commerce or Revenue to the Ports of one State over those of another; nor shall Vessels bound to, or from, one State, be obliged to enter, clear, or pay Duties in another.

No Money shall be drawn from the Treasury, but in Consequence of Appropriations made by Law; and a regular Statement and Account of the Receipts and Expenditures of all public Money shall be published from time to time.

No Title of Nobility shall be granted by the United States: And no Person holding any Office of Profit or Trust under them, shall, without the Consent of the Congress, accept of any present, Emolument, Office, or Title, of any kind whatever, from any King, Prince, or foreign State.

Section. 10.

No State shall enter into any Treaty, Alliance, or Confederation; grant Letters of Marque and Reprisal; coin Money; emit Bills of Credit; make any Thing but gold and silver Coin a Tender in Payment of Debts; pass any Bill of Attainder, ex post facto Law, or Law impairing the Obligation of Contracts, or grant any Title of Nobility.

No State shall, without the Consent of the Congress, lay any Imposts or Duties on Imports or Exports, except what may be absolutely necessary for executing it's inspection Laws: and the net Produce of all Duties and Imposts, laid by any State on Imports or Exports, shall be for the Use of the Treasury of the United States; and all such Laws shall be subject to the Revision and Controul of the Congress.

No State shall, without the Consent of Congress, lay any Duty of Tonnage, keep Troops, or Ships of War in time of Peace, enter into any Agreement or Compact with another State, or with a foreign Power, or engage in War, unless actually invaded, or in such imminent Danger as will not admit of delay.

Article. II.

Section. 1.

The executive Power shall be vested in a President of the United States of America. He shall hold his Office during the Term of four Years, and, together with the Vice President, chosen for the same Term, be elected, as follows:

Each State shall appoint, in such Manner as the Legislature thereof may direct, a Number of Electors, equal to the whole Number of Senators and Representatives to which the State may be entitled in the Congress: but no Senator or Representative, or Person holding an

Office of Trust or Profit under the United States, shall be appointed an Elector.

The Electors shall meet in their respective States, and vote by Ballot for two Persons, of whom one at least shall not be an Inhabitant of the same State with themselves. And they shall make a List of all the Persons voted for, and of the Number of Votes for each; which List they shall sign and certify, and transmit sealed to the Seat of the Government of the United States, directed to the President of the Senate. The President of the Senate shall, in the Presence of the Senate and House of Representatives, open all the Certificates, and the Votes shall then be counted. The Person having the greatest Number of Votes shall be the President, if such Number be a Majority of the whole Number of Electors appointed; and if there be more than one who have such Majority, and have an equal Number of Votes, then the House of Representatives shall immediately chuse by Ballot one of them for President; and if no Person have a Majority, then from the five highest on the List the said House shall in like Manner chuse the President. But in chusing the President, the Votes shall be taken by States, the Representation from each State having one Vote; A quorum for this purpose shall consist of a Member or Members from two thirds of the States, and a Majority of all the States shall be necessary to a Choice. In every Case, after the Choice of the President, the Person having the greatest Number of Votes of the Electors shall be the Vice President. But if there should remain two or more who have equal Votes, the Senate shall chuse from them by Ballot the Vice President.

The Congress may determine the Time of chusing the Electors, and the Day on which they shall give their Votes; which Day shall be the same throughout the United States.

No Person except a natural born Citizen, or a Citizen of the United States, at the time of the Adoption of this Constitution, shall be eligible to the Office of President; neither shall any Person be eligible to that Office who shall not have attained to the Age of thirty five Years, and been fourteen Years a Resident within the United States.

In Case of the Removal of the President from Office, or of his Death, Resignation, or Inability to discharge the Powers and Duties of the said Office, the Same shall devolve on the Vice President, and the Congress may by Law provide for the Case of Removal, Death, Resignation or Inability, both of the President and Vice President, declaring what Officer shall then act as President, and such Officer shall act accordingly, until the Disability be removed, or a President shall be elected.

The President shall, at stated Times, receive for his Services, a Compensation, which shall neither be increased nor diminished during the Period for which he shall have been elected, and he shall not receive within that Period any other Emolument from the United States, or any of them.

Before he enter on the Execution of his Office, he shall take the following Oath or Affirmation:--"I do solemnly swear (or affirm) that I will faithfully execute the Office of President of the United States, and will to the best of my Ability, preserve, protect and defend the Constitution of the United States."

Section. 2.

The President shall be Commander in Chief of the Army and Navy of the United States, and of the Militia of the several States, when called into the actual Service of the United States; he may require the Opinion, in writing, of the principal Officer in each of the executive Departments, upon any Subject relating to the Duties of their respective Offices, and he shall have Power to grant Reprieves and Pardons for Offences against the United States, except in Cases of Impeachment.

He shall have Power, by and with the Advice and Consent of the Senate, to make Treaties, provided two thirds of the Senators present concur; and he shall nominate, and by and with the Advice and Consent of the Senate, shall appoint Ambassadors, other public Ministers and Consuls, Judges of the supreme Court, and all other Officers of the United States, whose Appointments are not herein otherwise provided for, and which shall be established by Law: but the Congress may by Law vest the Appointment of such inferior Officers, as they think proper, in the President alone, in the Courts of Law, or in the Heads of Departments.

The President shall have Power to fill up all Vacancies that may happen during the Recess of the Senate, by granting Commissions which shall expire at the End of their next Session.

Section. 3.

He shall from time to time give to the Congress Information of the State of the Union, and recommend to their Consideration such Measures as he shall judge necessary and expedient; he may, on extraordinary Occasions, convene both Houses, or either of them, and in Case of Disagreement between them, with Respect to the Time of Adjournment, he may adjourn them to such Time as he shall think proper; he shall receive Ambassadors and other public Ministers; he shall take Care that the Laws be faithfully executed, and shall Commission all the Officers of the United States.

Section. 4.

The President, Vice President and all civil Officers of the United States, shall be removed from Office on Impeachment for, and Conviction of, Treason, Bribery, or other high Crimes and Misdemeanors.

Article III.
Section. 1.

The judicial Power of the United States shall be vested in one supreme Court, and in such inferior Courts as the Congress may from time to time ordain and establish. The Judges, both of the supreme and inferior Courts, shall hold their Offices during good Behaviour, and shall, at stated Times, receive for their Services a Compensation, which shall not be diminished during their Continuance in Office.

Section. 2.

The judicial Power shall extend to all Cases, in Law and Equity, arising under this Constitution, the Laws of the United States, and Treaties made, or which shall be made, under their Authority;--to all Cases affecting Ambassadors, other public Ministers and Consuls;--to all Cases of admiralty and maritime Jurisdiction;--to Controversies to which the United States shall be a Party;--to Controversies between two or more States;-- between a State and Citizens of another State,--between Citizens of different States,--between Citizens of the same State claiming Lands under Grants of different States, and between a State, or the Citizens thereof, and foreign States, Citizens or Subjects.

In all Cases affecting Ambassadors, other public Ministers and Consuls, and those in which a State shall be Party, the supreme Court shall have original Jurisdiction. In all the other Cases before mentioned, the supreme Court shall have appellate Jurisdiction, both as to Law and Fact, with such Exceptions, and under such Regulations as the Congress shall make.

The Trial of all Crimes, except in Cases of Impeachment, shall be by Jury; and such Trial shall be held in the State where the said Crimes shall have been committed; but when not committed within any State, the Trial shall be at such Place or Places as the Congress may by Law have directed.

Section. 3.

Treason against the United States, shall consist only in levying War against them, or in adhering to their Enemies, giving them Aid and Comfort. No Person shall be convicted of Treason unless on the Testimony of two Witnesses to the same overt Act, or on Confession in open Court.

The Congress shall have Power to declare the Punishment of

Treason, but no Attainder of Treason shall work Corruption of Blood, or Forfeiture except during the Life of the Person attainted.

Article. IV.
Section. 1.

Full Faith and Credit shall be given in each State to the public Acts, Records, and judicial Proceedings of every other State. And the Congress may by general Laws prescribe the Manner in which such Acts, Records and Proceedings shall be proved, and the Effect thereof.

Section. 2.

The Citizens of each State shall be entitled to all Privileges and Immunities of Citizens in the several States.

A Person charged in any State with Treason, Felony, or other Crime, who shall flee from Justice, and be found in another State, shall on Demand of the executive Authority of the State from which he fled, be delivered up, to be removed to the State having Jurisdiction of the Crime.

No Person held to Service or Labour in one State, under the Laws thereof, escaping into another, shall, in Consequence of any Law or Regulation therein, be discharged from such Service or Labour, but shall be delivered up on Claim of the Party to whom such Service or Labour may be due.

Section. 3.

New States may be admitted by the Congress into this Union; but no new State shall be formed or erected within the Jurisdiction of any other State; nor any State be formed by the Junction of two or more States, or Parts of States, without the Consent of the Legislatures of the States concerned as well as of the Congress.

The Congress shall have Power to dispose of and make all needful Rules and Regulations respecting the Territory or other Property belonging to the United States; and nothing in this Constitution shall be so construed as to Prejudice any Claims of the United States, or of any particular State.

Section. 4.

The United States shall guarantee to every State in this Union a Republican Form of Government, and shall protect each of them against Invasion; and on Application of the Legislature, or of the Executive (when the Legislature cannot be convened), against domestic Violence.

Article. V.

The Congress, whenever two thirds of both Houses shall deem it necessary, shall propose Amendments to this Constitution, or, on the Application of the Legislatures of two thirds of the several States, shall call a Convention for proposing Amendments, which, in either Case, shall be valid to all Intents and Purposes, as Part of this Constitution, when ratified by the Legislatures of three fourths of the several States, or by Conventions in three fourths thereof, as the one or the other Mode of Ratification may be proposed by the Congress; Provided that no Amendment which may be made prior to the Year One thousand eight hundred and eight shall in any Manner affect the first and fourth Clauses in the Ninth Section of the first Article; and that no State, without its Consent, shall be deprived of its equal Suffrage in the Senate.

Article. VI.

All Debts contracted and Engagements entered into, before the Adoption of this Constitution, shall be as valid against the United States under this Constitution, as under the Confederation.

This Constitution, and the Laws of the United States which shall be made in Pursuance thereof; and all Treaties made, or which shall be made, under the Authority of the United States, shall be the supreme Law of the Land; and the Judges in every State shall be bound thereby, any Thing in the Constitution or Laws of any State to the Contrary notwithstanding.

The Senators and Representatives before mentioned, and the Members of the several State Legislatures, and all executive and judicial Officers, both of the United States and of the several States, shall be bound by Oath or Affirmation, to support this Constitution; but no religious Test shall ever be required as a Qualification to any Office or public Trust under the United States.

Article. VII.

The ratification of the conventions of nine States shall be sufficient for the establishment of this Constitution between the States so ratifying the same.

DONE in convention by the unanimous consent of the States present the seventeenth day of September in the Year of our Lord one thousand seven hundred and eighty seven, and of the independence of the United States of America the twelfth.

Signers of the Constitution

DELAWARE: George Read, Gunning Bedford, Jr., John Dickinson, Richard Bassett, Jacob Broom

MARYLAND: James McHenry, Daniel of St. Thomas Jenifer, Daniel Carroll

VIRGINIA: John Blair, James Madison, Jr., George Washington

NORTH CAROLINA: William Blount, Richard Dobbs Spaight, Hugh Williamson

SOUTH CAROLINA: John Rutledge, Charles Cotesworth Pinckney, Charles Pinckney, Pierce Butler

GEORGIA: William Few, Abraham Baldwin

NEW HAMPSHIRE: John Langdon, Nicholas Gilman
MASSACHUSETTS: Nathaniel Gorham, Rufus King
CONNECTICUT: William Samuel Johnson, Roger Sherman
NEW YORK: Alexander Hamilton
NEW JERSEY: William Livingston, David Brearley, William Paterson, Jonathan Dayton
PENNSYLVANIA: Benjamin Franklin, Thomas Mifflin, Robert Morris, George Clymer, Thomas Fitzsimons, Jared Ingersoll, James Wilson, Gouverneur Morris

The Transcription of the Bill of Rights: The Bill of Rights includes the first ten amendments to the Constitution.

The Preamble to The Bill of Rights

Congress of the United States begun and held at the City of New-York, on Wednesday the fourth of March, one thousand seven hundred and eighty nine.

THE Conventions of a number of the States, having at the time of their adopting the Constitution, expressed a desire, in order to prevent misconstruction or abuse of its powers, that further declaratory and restrictive clauses should be added: And as extending the ground of public confidence in the Government, will best ensure the beneficent ends of its institution.

RESOLVED by the Senate and House of Representatives of the United States of America, in Congress assembled, two thirds of both Houses concurring, that the following Articles be proposed to the Legislatures of the several States, as amendments to the Constitution of the United States, all, or any of which Articles, when ratified by three fourths of the said Legislatures, to be valid to all intents and purposes, as part of the said Constitution; viz.

ARTICLES in addition to, and Amendment of the Constitution of the United States of America, proposed by Congress, and ratified by the Legislatures of the several States, pursuant to the fifth Article of the original Constitution.

Amendment I

Congress shall make no law respecting an establishment of religion, or prohibiting the free exercise thereof; or abridging the freedom of speech, or of the press; or the right of the people peaceably to assemble, and to petition the Government for a redress of grievances.

Amendment II

A well regulated Militia, being necessary to the security of a free State, the right of the people to keep and bear Arms, shall not be infringed.

Amendment III

No Soldier shall, in time of peace be quartered in any house, without the consent of the Owner, nor in time of war, but in a manner to be prescribed by law.

Amendment IV

The right of the people to be secure in their persons, houses, papers, and effects, against unreasonable searches and seizures, shall not be violated, and no Warrants shall issue, but upon probable cause, supported by Oath or affirmation, and particularly describing the place to be searched, and the persons or things to be seized.

Amendment V

No person shall be held to answer for a capital, or otherwise infamous crime, unless on a presentment or indictment of a Grand Jury, except in cases arising in the land or naval forces, or in the Militia, when in actual service in time of War or public danger; nor shall any person be subject for the same offence to be twice put in jeopardy of life or limb; nor shall be compelled in any criminal case to be a witness against himself, nor be deprived of life, liberty, or property, without due process of law; nor shall private property be taken for public use, without just compensation.

Amendment VI

In all criminal prosecutions, the accused shall enjoy the right to a speedy and public trial, by an impartial jury of the State and district wherein the crime shall have been committed, which district shall have been previously ascertained by law, and to be informed of the nature and cause of the accusation; to be confronted with the witnesses against him; to have compulsory process for obtaining witnesses in his favor, and to have the Assistance of Counsel for his defence.

Amendment VII

In Suits at common law, where the value in controversy shall exceed twenty dollars, the right of trial by jury shall be preserved, and no fact tried by a jury, shall be otherwise re-examined in any Court of the United States, than according to the rules of the common law.

Amendment VIII

Excessive bail shall not be required, nor excessive fines imposed, nor cruel and unusual punishments inflicted.

Amendment IX

The enumeration in the Constitution, of certain rights, shall not be construed to deny or disparage others retained by the people.

Amendment X

The powers not delegated to the United States by the Constitution, nor prohibited by it to the States, are reserved to the States respectively, or to the people.

The Transcription of the Original Amendments Eleven through Twenty-Seven

AMENDMENT XI
Passed by Congress March 4, 1794. Ratified February 7, 1795.
Note: Article III, section 2, of the Constitution was modified by amendment 11.

The Judicial power of the United States shall not be construed to extend to any suit in law or equity, commenced or prosecuted against one of the United States by Citizens of another State, or by Citizens or Subjects of any Foreign State.

AMENDMENT XII
Passed by Congress December 9, 1803. Ratified June 15, 1804.
Note: A portion of Article II, section 1 of the Constitution was superseded by the 12th amendment.

The Electors shall meet in their respective states and vote by ballot for President and Vice-President, one of whom, at least, shall not be an inhabitant of the same state with themselves; they shall name in their ballots the person voted for as President, and in distinct ballots the person voted for as Vice-President, and they shall make distinct lists of all persons voted for as President, and of all persons voted for as Vice-President, and of the number of votes for each, which lists they shall sign and certify, and transmit sealed to the seat of the government of the United States, directed to the President of the Senate; -- the

President of the Senate shall, in the presence of the Senate and House of Representatives, open all the certificates and the votes shall then be counted; -- The person having the greatest number of votes for President, shall be the President, if such number be a majority of the whole number of Electors appointed; and if no person have such majority, then from the persons having the highest numbers not exceeding three on the list of those voted for as President, the House of Representatives shall choose immediately, by ballot, the President. But in choosing the President, the votes shall be taken by states, the representation from each state having one vote; a quorum for this purpose shall consist of a member or members from two-thirds of the states, and a majority of all the states shall be necessary to a choice. [And if the House of Representatives shall not choose a President whenever the right of choice shall devolve upon them, before the fourth day of March next following, then the Vice-President shall act as President, as in case of the death or other constitutional disability of the President. --]* The person having the greatest number of votes as Vice-President, shall be the Vice-President, if such number be a majority of the whole number of Electors appointed, and if no person have a majority, then from the two highest numbers on the list, the Senate shall choose the Vice-President; a quorum for the purpose shall consist of two-thirds of the whole number of Senators, and a majority of the whole number shall be necessary to a choice. But no person constitutionally ineligible to the office of President shall be eligible to that of Vice-President of the United States.

*Superseded by section 3 of the 20th amendment.

AMENDMENT XIII

Passed by Congress January 31, 1865. Ratified December 6, 1865.

Note: A portion of Article IV, section 2, of the Constitution was superseded by the 13th amendment.

Section 1.

Neither slavery nor involuntary servitude, except as a punishment for crime whereof the party shall have been duly convicted, shall exist within the United States, or any place subject to their jurisdiction.

Section 2.

Congress shall have power to enforce this article by appropriate legislation.

AMENDMENT XIV

Passed by Congress June 13, 1866. Ratified July 9, 1868.
Note: Article I, section 2, of the Constitution was modified by section 2 of the 14th amendment.

Section 1.

All persons born or naturalized in the United States, and subject to the jurisdiction thereof, are citizens of the United States and of the State wherein they reside. No State shall make or enforce any law which shall abridge the privileges or immunities of citizens of the United States; nor shall any State deprive any person of life, liberty, or property, without due process of law; nor deny to any person within its jurisdiction the equal protection of the laws.

Section 2.

Representatives shall be apportioned among the several States according to their respective numbers, counting the whole number of persons in each State, excluding Indians not taxed. But when the right to vote at any election for the choice of electors for President and Vice-President of the United States, Representatives in Congress, the Executive and Judicial officers of a State, or the members of the Legislature thereof, is denied to any of the male inhabitants of such State, being twenty-one years of age,* and citizens of the United States, or in any way abridged, except for participation in rebellion, or other crime, the basis of representation therein shall be reduced in the proportion which the number of such male citizens shall bear to the whole number of male citizens twenty-one years of age in such State.

Section 3.

No person shall be a Senator or Representative in Congress, or elector of President and Vice-President, or hold any office, civil or military, under the United States, or under any State, who, having previously taken an oath, as a member of Congress, or as an officer of the United States, or as a member of any State legislature, or as an executive or judicial officer of any State, to support the Constitution of the United States, shall have engaged in insurrection or rebellion against the same, or given aid or comfort to the enemies thereof. But Congress may by a vote of two-thirds of each House, remove such disability.

Section 4.

The validity of the public debt of the United States, authorized by law, including debts incurred for payment of pensions and bounties for services in suppressing insurrection or rebellion, shall not be questioned. But neither the United States nor any State shall assume or pay any debt or obligation incurred in aid of insurrection or rebellion against the United States, or any claim for the loss or emancipation of any slave; but all such debts, obligations and claims shall be held illegal and void.

Section 5.

The Congress shall have the power to enforce, by appropriate legislation, the provisions of this article.

Changed by section 1 of the 26th amendment.
AMENDMENT XV
Passed by Congress February 26, 1869. Ratified February 3, 1870.
Section 1.

The right of citizens of the United States to vote shall not be denied or abridged by the United States or by any State on account of race, color, or previous condition of servitude--

Section 2.

The Congress shall have the power to enforce this article by appropriate legislation.

AMENDMENT XVI

Passed by Congress July 2, 1909. Ratified February 3, 1913.
Note: Article I, section 9, of the Constitution was modified by amendment 16.

The Congress shall have power to lay and collect taxes on incomes, from whatever source derived, without apportionment among the several States, and without regard to any census or enumeration.

AMENDMENT XVII

Passed by Congress May 13, 1912. Ratified April 8, 1913.
Note: Article I, section 3, of the Constitution was modified by the 17th amendment.

The Senate of the United States shall be composed of two Senators from each State, elected by the people thereof, for six years; and each Senator shall have one vote. The electors in each State shall have the qualifications requisite for electors of the most numerous branch of the State legislatures.

When vacancies happen in the representation of any State in the Senate, the executive authority of such State shall issue writs of election to fill such vacancies: *Provided*, That the legislature of any State may empower the executive thereof to make temporary appointments until the people fill the vacancies by election as the legislature may direct.

This amendment shall not be so construed as to affect the election or term of any Senator chosen before it becomes valid as part of the Constitution.

AMENDMENT XVIII

Passed by Congress December 18, 1917. Ratified January 16, 1919.
Repealed by amendment 21.

Section 1.

After one year from the ratification of this article the manufacture, sale, or transportation of intoxicating liquors within, the importation thereof into, or the exportation thereof from the United States and all territory subject to the jurisdiction thereof for beverage purposes is hereby prohibited.

Section 2.

The Congress and the several States shall have concurrent power to enforce this article by appropriate legislation.

Section 3.

This article shall be inoperative unless it shall have been ratified as an amendment to the Constitution by the legislatures of the several States, as provided in the Constitution, within seven years from the date of the submission hereof to the States by the Congress.

AMENDMENT XIX

Passed by Congress June 4, 1919. Ratified August 18, 1920.

The right of citizens of the United States to vote shall not be denied or abridged by the United States or by any State on account of sex.

Congress shall have power to enforce this article by appropriate legislation.

AMENDMENT XX

Passed by Congress March 2, 1932. Ratified January 23, 1933.

Note: Article I, section 4, of the Constitution was modified by section 2 of this amendment. In addition, a portion of the 12th amendment was superseded by section 3.

Section 1.

The terms of the President and the Vice President shall end at noon on the 20th day of January, and the terms of Senators and Representatives at noon on the 3d day of January, of the years in which such terms would have ended if this article had not been ratified; and the terms of their successors shall then begin.

Section 2.

The Congress shall assemble at least once in every year, and such meeting shall begin at noon on the 3d day of January, unless they shall by law appoint a different day.

Section 3.

If, at the time fixed for the beginning of the term of the President, the President elect shall have died, the Vice President elect shall become President. If a President shall not have been chosen before the time fixed for the beginning of his term, or if the President elect shall have failed to qualify, then the Vice President elect shall act as President until a President shall have qualified; and the Congress may by law provide for the case wherein neither a President elect nor a Vice President shall have qualified, declaring who shall then act as President, or the manner in which one who is to act shall be selected, and such person shall act accordingly until a President or Vice President shall have qualified.

Section 4.

The Congress may by law provide for the case of the death of any of the persons from whom the House of Representatives may choose a President whenever the right of choice shall have devolved upon them, and for the case of the death of any of the persons from whom the Senate may choose a Vice President whenever the right of choice shall have devolved upon them.

Section 5.

Sections 1 and 2 shall take effect on the 15th day of October following the ratification of this article.

Section 6.

This article shall be inoperative unless it shall have been ratified as an amendment to the Constitution by the legislatures of three-fourths of the several States within seven years from the date of its submission.

AMENDMENT XXI
Passed by Congress February 20, 1933. Ratified December 5, 1933.
Section 1.
The eighteenth article of amendment to the Constitution of the United States is hereby repealed.

Section 2.
The transportation or importation into any State, Territory, or Possession of the United States for delivery or use therein of intoxicating liquors, in violation of the laws thereof, is hereby prohibited.

Section 3.
This article shall be inoperative unless it shall have been ratified as an amendment to the Constitution by conventions in the several States, as provided in the Constitution, within seven years from the date of the submission hereof to the States by the Congress.

AMENDMENT XXII
Passed by Congress March 21, 1947. Ratified February 27, 1951.
Section 1.
No person shall be elected to the office of the President more than twice, and no person who has held the office of President, or acted as President, for more than two years of a term to which some other person was elected President shall be elected to the office of President more than once. But this Article shall not apply to any person holding the office of President when this Article was proposed by Congress, and shall not prevent any person who may be holding the office of President, or acting as President, during the term within which this

Article becomes operative from holding the office of President or acting as President during the remainder of such term.

Section 2.

This article shall be inoperative unless it shall have been ratified as an amendment to the Constitution by the legislatures of three-fourths of the several States within seven years from the date of its submission to the States by the Congress.

AMENDMENT XXIII

Passed by Congress June 16, 1960. Ratified March 29, 1961.

Section 1.

The District constituting the seat of Government of the United States shall appoint in such manner as Congress may direct:

A number of electors of President and Vice President equal to the whole number of Senators and Representatives in Congress to which the District would be entitled if it were a State, but in no event more than the least populous State; they shall be in addition to those appointed by the States, but they shall be considered, for the purposes of the election of President and Vice President, to be electors appointed by a State; and they shall meet in the District and perform such duties as provided by the twelfth article of amendment.

Section 2.

The Congress shall have power to enforce this article by appropriate legislation.

AMENDMENT XXIV

Passed by Congress August 27, 1962. Ratified January 23, 1964.

Section 1.

The right of citizens of the United States to vote in any primary or other election for President or Vice President, for electors for President or Vice President, or for Senator or Representative in Congress, shall not be denied or abridged by the United States or any State by reason of failure to pay poll tax or other tax.

Section 2.

The Congress shall have power to enforce this article by appropriate legislation.

AMENDMENT XXV

Passed by Congress July 6, 1965. Ratified February 10, 1967.
Note: Article II, section 1, of the Constitution was affected by the 25th amendment.

Section 1.

In case of the removal of the President from office or of his death or resignation, the Vice President shall become President.

Section 2.

Whenever there is a vacancy in the office of the Vice President, the President shall nominate a Vice President who shall take office upon confirmation by a majority vote of both Houses of Congress.

Section 3.

Whenever the President transmits to the President pro tempore of the Senate and the Speaker of the House of Representatives his written declaration that he is unable to discharge the powers and duties of his office, and until he transmits to them a written declaration to the contrary, such powers and duties shall be discharged by the Vice President as Acting President.

Section 4.

Whenever the Vice President and a majority of either the principal officers of the executive departments or of such other body as Congress may by law provide, transmit to the President pro tempore of the Senate and the Speaker of the House of Representatives their written declaration that the President is unable to discharge the powers and duties of his office, the Vice President shall immediately assume the powers and duties of the office as Acting President.

Thereafter, when the President transmits to the President pro tempore of the Senate and the Speaker of the House of Representatives his written declaration that no inability exists, he shall resume the powers and duties of his office unless the Vice President and a majority of either the principal officers of the executive department or of such other body as Congress may by law provide, transmit within four days to the President pro tempore of the Senate and the Speaker of the House of Representatives their written declaration that the President is unable to discharge the powers and duties of his office. Thereupon Congress shall decide the issue, assembling within forty-eight hours for that purpose if not in session. If the Congress, within twenty-one days after receipt of the latter written declaration, or, if Congress is not in session, within twenty-one days after Congress is required to assemble, determines by two-thirds vote of both Houses that the President is unable to discharge the powers and duties of his office, the Vice President shall continue to discharge the same as Acting President; otherwise, the President shall resume the powers and duties of his office.

AMENDMENT XXVI
Passed by Congress March 23, 1971. Ratified July 1, 1971.
Note: Amendment 14, section 2, of the Constitution was modified by section 1 of the 26th amendment.
Section 1.
The right of citizens of the United States, who are eighteen years of age or older, to vote shall not be denied or abridged by the United States or by any State on account of age.

Section 2.
The Congress shall have power to enforce this article by appropriate legislation.

AMENDMENT XXVII

Originally proposed <u>Sept. 25, 1789</u>. Ratified May 7, 1992.

No law, varying the compensation for the services of the Senators and Representatives, shall take effect, until an election of representatives shall have intervened.

Patriotic Pictures and Posts for Facebook and Other Social Media

Visit **Unite the USA** on Facebook to see dozens of "postcards" with a purpose. We call them that because they are pictures with a message of truth to help spread the word about what's really happened or is happening in our country. Be an online Paul (or Paulette) Revere! Spread the truth in a way people can see and relate so that they are activated.

How to Post on Facebook Pages:
1. *Right-click on one of our Facebook pictures found in the "Timeline Album."*
2. *Click on the photo of your choice and select "Save Picture As" so that you can then save it on your computer as a picture.*
3. *Finally, follow the Facebook instructions to post a picture on your page. Yes, it's that simple to spread the message!*

How to Contact Congress

Every citizen's duty is to interact with and encourage elected officials to adhere to the U.S. Constitution. Important contact information for U.S. Senators and Representatives can be found at the following online locations:

- U.S. Senators can be contacted at http://www.senate.gov/general/contact_information/senators_cfm.cfm.
- U.S. Representatives can be contacted at http://www.house.gov/representatives/find/.

Take God's Word for It by Stacie Ruth

Devotionals to Inspire the Nation to Look to God for Salvation

One: "Security for Insecure Times"

You can't talk to terrorists. They'll shoot you. But you can have peace through strength. Yes, that's a theme for many in America. Ronald Reagan often talked about such a strategy. But it also holds true Scripturally: When you draw peace from having Jesus as your strength, you win. I thank God for a great example of that:

"Grandma Hilda" possessed great peace through the Lord's strength. She joined the Lord at 98 ½ years old. Grandma Hilda walked with Jesus for a long time. She loved Him! Even with dementia, she liked to sing "Jesus Loves Me" with me. Grandma lives in Heaven with eternal security because of our ever-victorious Lord Jesus, who will right all things in the end!

Grandma Hilda, whose unconditional love and realness reflected Christ, would want me to ask you this: Do you know that you're a secure citizen of Heaven who will go there when you die? Do you know Jesus personally? When you know Jesus, you can "take God's Word for it": "But our citizenship is in heaven, and from it we await a Savior, the Lord Jesus Christ, who will transform our lowly body to be like his glorious body, by the power that enables him even to subject all things to himself" (Ephesians 3:20-21).

Two: "Just Jesus!"

To start, take God's Word for it: "Those who look to him are radiant, and their faces shall never be ashamed" (Ps. 34:5). Today, we each must ask the Lord Jesus, "Am I radiating Your love and light?" I pray so. Let's ask the Lord to help us shine for His glory and His alone! We're to point people not to our own appearance but rather to His. He came! And He's coming again!

Let's pray together and ask Him to help us live like we believe He's coming...because He is! "Lord, we love You. We ask for your forgiveness for relying on other things instead of You at all times. We repent. We trust in You. Please shine through us, Jesus. Please use us. We look to You and You alone! In Jesus' Name, Amen."

It's time to stop thinking about how we're coming off with other people instead of how we're shining Christ's light and love. May people see just Jesus in me! That's my prayer.

Take God's Word for It: "May the grace of the Lord Jesus Christ, the love of God, and the fellowship of the Holy Spirit be with you all." --2 Corinthians 13:14

Three: "Stressed Out? Be Blessed."

Stressed out? Let the Lord Jesus lead you beside quiet waters, restore your soul, and comfort you... Today, savor Ps. 23:1 with me: "The Lord is my Shepherd [to feed, guide, and shield me], I shall not lack." In the New Testament (John 10:11, AMP), Jesus said, "I am the Good Shepherd. The Good Shepherd risks and lays down His [own] life for the sheep."

When we receive Jesus, we receive everything we need: He is the ultimate answer to all our hearts' cries. He holds us when others despise. And it's His blood that sanctifies...Jesus. Our good Shepherd... Be blessed as you lean on Him.

Let's pray: "Lord Jesus, we thank You for being such a good shepherd and that we lack nothing when You are our everything.

Please forgive us for using other things to satisfy. Lord, we welcome You in our hearts and lives. In Jesus' Name, Amen."

Take God's Word for it: "Greater love has no one than this, that someone lay down his life for his friends."--Jesus Christ, our good Shepherd (See John 15:13.)

Four: "Give your storm to Jesus.
He alone gives perfect peacefulness."

Do you feel like your personal storm is so harsh that the rain feels like needles and you can't fight it anymore? Trade your storm for Jesus' peace. He speaks peace and offers still waters -not crushing, crashing waves.

Today, savor Ps. 23:2 with me: "He makes me lie down in [fresh, tender] green pastures; He leads me beside the still and restful waters." In the New Testament (Mark 4:39, AMP), we see Jesus can make the most turbulent waters still and peaceful: "And He arose and rebuked the wind and said to the sea, Hush now! Be still (muzzled)! And the wind ceased (sank to rest as if exhausted by its beating) and there was [immediately] a great calm (a perfect peacefulness)."

Perfect peacefulness. That's what Jesus provides. As a little girl, I wrote a song about it. As a young lady, I still believe it. I've experienced it. Peace... Perfect peacefulness in Jesus.

Let's pray: "Lord Jesus, we thank You that You are more powerful than any storm we feel. And we thank You that in You we can have 'perfect peacefulness'. We welcome You in our hearts. We repent from analyzing too much. With child-like dependence, we lean hard on You today. Thank You for being You! In Jesus' Name, Amen."

Take God's Word for it: "And He arose and rebuked the wind and said to the sea, Hush now! Be still (muzzled)! And the wind ceased (sank to rest as if exhausted by its beating) and there was [immediately] a great calm (a perfect peacefulness).".--Jesus Christ, our good Shepherd (See Mark 4:39.)

Five: "Jesus Refreshes"

The heated politics in the United States reveal a profound need for people to forsake hatred and start loving God and fellow man. Many folks simply feel stressed out by the economy, moral conditions of our country, etc. But no stress -including national stressors- exceeds God's ability to refresh.

No pain exceeds Jesus' ability to alleviate. (Yes, that includes your painful, stressful situation you can't seem to shake off.)

No matter the source of your stress and heartache, you can count on Christ. Today, savor Ps. 23:3a (AMP) with me: "He refreshes and restores my life (my self)..." In the New Testament, Jesus lovingly offered true refreshment with these words: "Come to Me, all you who labor and are heavy-laden and overburdened, and I will cause you to rest. [I will ease and relieve and refresh your souls.]" (Matthew 11:28, AMP)

Let's pray: "Lord Jesus, we confess our desperate need of You and Your refreshment. We are sorry for running away from You instead of running to You at all times...especially stressful times. We welcome You afresh in our hearts and ask You to refresh us in the deepest places of our hearts. We love You, Lord. We give You our hearts, souls, minds, and strength and ask that, with those, we would love You fully as You so fully love us. In Jesus' Name, Amen."

Take God's Word for it: "So repent (change your mind and purpose); turn around and return [to God], that your sins may be erased (blotted out, wiped clean), that times of refreshing (of recovering from the effects of heat, of reviving with fresh air) may come from the presence of the Lord..."-Acts 3:19, AMP

Six: "The Lord loves on us as He leads us."

Someone reading this is feeling close to despair. It's okay: You're not alone. Just trust Jesus. He said, "I am with you always..." And that includes right now. You're going to win with His help! Just trust Him... rest in Him. He leads and provides for our needs.

Today, I saw a little girl running around with curls bouncing. I glanced around: No one seemed to be leading her. So I watched until I knew she was safe. Unfortunately, her guardian had failed to do her job well.

But Jesus never misleads us. He loves on us and leads us every single day! Today, let's savor how our Lord fulfills Ps. 23:3b (AMP): "He leads me in the paths of righteousness [uprightness and right standing with Him-not for my earning it, but] for His name's sake."

In the New Testament, Jesus lovingly reminded us that He knows how to communicate with us and keep us even as He leads us: "The sheep that are My own hear and are listening to My voice; and I know them, and they follow Me. And I give them eternal life, and they shall never lose it or perish throughout the ages. [To all eternity they shall never by any means be destroyed.] And no one is able to snatch them out of My hand" (John 10:27-28).

Let's pray: "Lord Jesus, we thank You for Your constant keeping of us. We entrust our entire lives to You afresh. We lean on You alone for salvation and listen to Your voice right now. We ask You to help us tune out the world and tune into You alone. We worship You on Your holy throne! In Jesus' Name, Amen."

Take God's Word for It: "The sheep that are My own hear and are listening to My voice; and I know them, and they follow Me."-Jesus, as in John 10:27 (AMP)

Seven: "Jesus keeps us safe."

Time and again I hear about people who tried "fitting in" with the trends of today...drinking, using drugs, premarital sex, etc. I hear about how they tried it all yet still felt sad deep down inside...like something or Someone was missing.

Then Jesus came to them and life transformed into abundant living! I mean, completely transformed! Countless testimonies worldwide attest to the life-giving, life-changing moment when people let Jesus inside. He is the way, the truth, and the life! His love casts out fear! And He's always there (unlike many people who fail you). When life's tough here, the biggest difference of all is knowing that Jesus is there and final victory remains secure in Him.

Jesus keeps us safe. He destroys our worst fears and creates us anew. The sting of death and fear disappears.

Fears can really interfere with our lives. It can be fierce when misdirected. But, if we fear (respect and revere) God, we don't need to experience the awful forms of fear in our lives because we trust Him to protect us from evil. Today, let's savor how our Lord fulfills Ps. 23:4a (AMP): "Yes, though I walk through the [deep, sunless] valley of the shadow of death, I will fear or dread no evil, for You are with me..."

In the New Testament, Jesus reminds us tenderly and joyously that He gives us life abundantly: "The thief comes only to steal and kill and destroy. I came that they may have life and have it abundantly." (John 10:10)

Yes! Jesus keeps us safe! No evil can stop us from going to Heaven when we die. God's love flattens our worst fears. Hallelujah! What a Savior!

Let's pray: "Lord Jesus, thank You for keeping us safe from evil. We entrust our entire lives to You afresh. We lean on You alone for salvation and listen to Your voice right now. We ask You to help us tune out the world and tune into You alone. We love You! In Jesus' Name, Amen."

Take God's Word for it: "The thief comes only to steal and kill and destroy. I came that they may have life and have it abundantly." (John 10:10)

Eight: "The Comfort of Christ"

A lot of stress and trials continue to assail America. Isn't it time we all turn to God in this crazy, imperfect world? It's clear: This world needs a Savior. His Name is Jesus Christ.

The Lord SO loves you. And He responds so graciously to repentance (of sin) and acceptance (of His Son). Nothing compares to His love! He alone gives eternal life: "For God so loved the world that he gave his one and only Son, that whoever believes in him shall not perish but have eternal life" (John 3:16).

Is your heart troubled yet you paint a smile across your face? Do you need comfort, direction, and grace? The Lord sees you and loves you so. Let the Lord hold you close. Don't turn away from God. Instead, turn to Him now.

Today, let's savor how our Lord Jesus fulfills Ps. 23:4 (AMP): "Yes, though I walk through the [deep, sunless] valley of the shadow of death, I will fear or dread no evil, for You are with me; Your rod [to protect] and Your staff [to guide], they comfort me." In the New Testament, Jesus said, "Let not your hearts be troubled. Believe in God; believe also in me" (John 14:1, ESV).

Think of it! Christ comforts us as He guides and protects us...all at once. He provides for every need.

Let's pray: "Heavenly Father, we thank You for being so willing to comfort us, lead us, and protect us...all at once! Our hearts need Your comfort today. You never fail to keep Your Word. We trust in You and You alone. Oh, thank You for comforting us! Thank You, Jesus, for being our Good Shepherd! In Jesus' Name, Amen."

Take God's Word for it: "Let not your hearts be troubled. Believe in God; believe also in me" (John 14:1, ESV).

Nine: "Jesus ministers to us –even in the presence of our enemies!"

Feel blown out of the water? I relate. A lot of folks feel that way because of various trials. But, sometimes, it takes a major blow to kick-start reliance upon God and a tremendous moving of His Spirit in the hearts of His people. **When you have nowhere to go but God, you go where you needed to be all the time.**

Hey, whoever said that being a Christian makes life easy was totally, 100% wrong. Fellow Christians, Jesus warned that we would have tribulation. But He also promised believers that He will be with us and we will be with Him for eternity! That makes a 100% difference! Jesus: "I have said these things to you, that in me you may have peace. In the world you will have tribulation. But take heart; I have overcome the world." (John 16:33) He can use us anywhere, anytime if we're willing to obey Him anywhere, anytime. In fact, He even ministers to our hearts' needs in the very presence of hate-filled enemies!

Today, let's savor how our Lord Jesus fulfills Ps. 23:5 (AMP): "You prepare a table before me in the presence of my enemies. You anoint my head with oil; my [brimming] cup runs over." In the New Testament, Jesus said, "A thief is only there to steal and kill and destroy. I came so they can have real and eternal life, more and better life than they ever dreamed of." (John 10:10).

Are you fearing the future? You don't have to! God will grant grace and provide for you in the moment of need...even in the presence of your enemies. And He will guide you! Isaiah 30:21 (AMP): "And your ears will hear a word behind you, saying, This is the way; walk in it, when you turn to the right hand and when you turn to the left."

Let's pray: "Heavenly Father, we love You and desire to be obedient children to whom You'll one day say, 'Well done.' Please help us help others to see You. Open doors for us to share the Gospel, please! We love You and thank You for Your love and for how You minister to us even in the presence of our enemies. In Jesus' Name, Amen."

Ten: Goodness and Mercy

"Surely goodness and mercy shall follow me all the days of my life, and I shall dwell in the house of the Lord forever."-Psalm 23:6

Each year, various annual holidays grant millions of American families an opportunity to gather and celebrate the Lord's faithfulness. Each year, many family tables include an empty chair.

In a friend's family, three loved ones perished within the last few months. And now another loved one has invasive brain cancer. The tears came yesterday at a gathering, but they took great comfort in Jesus and still thanked Him. You see, Jesus Christ is real and grants grace at time of need. He always comes through.

He came through for you on the cross. Oh, yes, this world includes much sorrow, sin, and pain. That's why Jesus came. He wants us to accept Him -not reject Him- because He alone offers eternal life. He alone can save us from the eternal separation from God.

He alone reaches out and offers you Himself as your substitute on the cross. He took capital punishment for your sins, your mistakes, your falling short of God's glory. The Ten Commandments present us with God's standards. Even if we break one, we've offended our holy Creator. So that's why, out of His great love, He fulfilled His requirement for punishment of evil by laying it all on Jesus, who chose to suffer in our place and offer eternal rescue and paradise to those who accept Him.

Wow. Wow! WOW! What a Savior! After we welcome Him as Savior and Lord of our repentant hearts, we follow Jesus and His goodness and mercy follows us! Even as we endure the pain of missing loved ones, we know that He fulfills Psalm 23:6 (ESV): "Surely goodness and mercy shall follow me all the days of my life, and I shall dwell in the house of the Lord forever."

What's more, the Lord Jesus promises to be with us always. That includes now! Praise Him! And, along with this promise, He gives us a purpose that, as we love God and neighbor, we share His rescue plan for the world: "Go therefore and make disciples of all nations, baptizing them in the name of the Father and of the Son and of the Holy Spirit, teaching them to observe all that I have commanded you. And behold, I am with you always, to the end of the age" (Matthew 28:19-20).

Let's pray: "Heavenly Father, we thank You for sending Jesus in our place. We fully accept His gift of eternal life: We repent of choosing sin instead of Your Son. We turn from sin and turn to Him now. Jesus, please be our Savior and Lord. We trust in You -not in what we do. Come into our lives...fill the empty chairs with a sense of Your constant, comforting presence. We believe and confess You as Lord and thank You for Your love. We love You, too! In Jesus' Name, Amen."

Take God's Word for it: "I have said these things to you, that in me you may have peace. In the world you will have tribulation. But take heart; I have overcome the world." (John 16:33)

Eleven: No Age Limits

Are you feeling old? Do you feel useless? God can use you at any age! Think about it: God never disqualifies people from service because of age. "Now Moses was 80 years old and Aaron 83 years old when they spoke to Pharaoh" (Exodus 7:7). Another image comes to mind: Daniel in the Lion's Den.

Did you realize that Daniel was approximately 85 years old at the time? Daniel prayed and obeyed. And God provided for him.

Whether you're old or young, you can be born again and forgiven of every sin. Be sure you know God personally: Get on God's side and let Jesus inside. He's the only Way to Heaven.

Celebrate the fact that Jesus said this: "All whom My Father gives (entrusts) to Me will come to Me; and the one who comes to Me I will most certainly not cast out [I will never, no never, reject one of them who comes to Me]" (John 6:37).

Take God's Word for it: "Now Moses was 80 years old and Aaron 83 years old when they spoke to Pharaoh" (Exodus 7:7).

Twelve: Answering the "Why" Question

"Why?" That question exits the lips of many who suffer here on earth. I confess that I have asked that question throughout tough times. Yet we must consider another question:

Why did Jesus suffer so much? That question is one that answers our "why" question of suffering. "But God demonstrates His own love toward us, in that while we were still sinners, Christ died for us" (Romans 5:8). He came to end the domain of darkness. When we know Him as Savior and Lord, we know that "He has delivered us from the domain of darkness and transferred us to the kingdom of his beloved Son, in whom we have redemption, the forgiveness of sins." (Colossians 1:13-14, ESV).

Before we continue this devotional, do you know Jesus as Savior and Lord? Learn more about how to know Him one-on-One and be able to conquer sin and death thru Him by visiting the "Know God" page on www.PrayingPals.org.

Also, sometimes the worst moments in our history present the best opportunities to give God glory and receive His gifts of mercy, grace, and eternal rewards. He feels our pain with us, and promises gain through Jesus. Let us remember Romans 8:18, which proclaims the truth that God is with us as we suffer, and promises the finest rewards hereafter: "[But what of that?] For I consider that the sufferings of this present time (this present life) are not worth being compared with the glory that is about to be revealed to us and in us and for us and conferred on us!" (AMP)

How do you overcome the "why" question and regain joy in the Lord Jesus? Realize and internalize the fact that suffering never indicates a change in God's goodness and His love for you. God loves you no matter what. Jesus got that point across when He hung naked, bleeding, suffering on the cross in your place...and in my place. But

He rose again and we who know Him personally will rise above every valley of pain!

Oh, what grace! Oh, what love! Take God's Word for it: "Nor height nor depth, nor anything else in all creation will be able to separate us from the love of God which is in Christ Jesus our Lord" (Romans 8:39, AMP).

Thirteen: "God's Love Remains the Same for You!"

I don't buy the prosperity gospel. You know, the whole "donate money and you'll be healed and wealthy" thing. Instead, I have great news! No matter what people say, this is true: Trials don't indicate that God suddenly ripped away His love from you. No way. He loves you just the same!

Take God's Word for it with me (Romans 5:1-5): "Therefore, since we have been justified by faith, we have peace with God through our Lord Jesus Christ. Through him we have also obtained access by faith into this grace in which we stand, and we rejoice in hope of the glory of God. Not only that, but we rejoice in our sufferings, knowing that suffering produces endurance, and endurance produces character, and character produces hope, and hope does not put us to shame, because God's love has been poured into our hearts through the Holy Spirit who has been given to us."

When you become a Christian, it doesn't guarantee a trouble-free life. Instead, when you know Jesus, you are given eternal wealth in Him! Such love! Such eternal security! Such peace and joy in spite of anything! When troubles come, He doesn't run. He sticks closer than a brother. Oh, nothing compares to Him!

You see, I know from experience: The cost of discipleship includes many trials, yet Jesus is with me for every mile. He carries me. He loves me. He holds me. And temporary trials on earth won't compare to the glories of eternity with Him in Heaven! I'd rather have Jesus than silver or gold. Find it hard to believe? Well, if you spend time with Jesus, you'll understand what I mean. Please! Get on God's Side:

Let Jesus inside your heart now. Later may not come. (If reading the e-book version, <u>click here to learn how to know God and go to Heaven</u>.)

Fourteen: Be an Overcomer in Christ!

"Well, I can't do anything more for you. You'll just have to push through the pain," a specialist coldly said to me. I paused before speaking. I prayed. Before I could speak much, the doctor had more to say: "I guess your pain is a 'Why God?' question."

My mouth dropped open a bit. Now, I hadn't expected that comment! So I said something like this: "Well, I know God is good and He is with me." He scoffed at my faith and left the room.

But Jesus didn't leave me. He's real no matter how we feel. Yes, we can get hit hard by unbelievers. But we can also experience pain upon pain because of misled believers.

You see, a trend in churches seems to convey that you just have to believe in order to receive anything you want...be it healing, money, relationships, whatever. Yes, as a Christian recording artist and author, I've traveled a lot and seen a wide range of churches.

Flamboyant, entertainment-driven churches give a false impression that the Christian life is easy here on earth. It's not. It's tough. But no trial compares to the fact of eternal security in Heaven with our beloved Lord.

I encourage you to remember this: In Christ, you're a guaranteed overcomer! Yes, for every believer, God's best is yet to come! Heaven is our home country and we'll spend eternity with the King of glory! Hallelujah!

Let's open our hearts to Jesus' words from John 16:33. **"These things I have spoken to you, that in Me you may have peace. In the world you will have tribulation; but be of good cheer, I have overcome the world."**

Share John 16:33 with someone else in pain. And, when you pray, praise the Lord for His 100% guaranteed victory in Christ!

Fifteen: God's Unstoppable Love

Take God's Word for it: "For I am persuaded that neither death nor life, nor angels nor principalities nor powers, nor things present nor things to come, nor height nor depth, nor any other created thing, shall be able to separate us from the love of God which is in Christ Jesus our Lord" (Romans 8:38-39).

Hallelujah! Praise the Lord! God's love never leaves us! I've shared about how the Lord helps me cope with physical pain. But I'm not doing so to complain or get attention. I'm sharing about it because I want to be real and tell you: Jesus' presence is "for real" and His presence has remained with me! I'm praying today that you sense His presence, too. Let's punch out the bad thoughts and whip out the sword of God's Word to overcome the enemy's distracting lies. It's time to focus on some Scripture and allow Scriptural truths to overcome emotional lies.

Myth: Pain indicates that God has reduced His love for you.
Fact: Pain never reflects a change in God's love for you! "For I am persuaded that neither death nor life, nor angels nor principalities nor powers, nor things present nor things to come, nor height nor depth, nor any other created thing, shall be able to separate us from the love of God which is in Christ Jesus our Lord" (Romans 8:38-39).

Sixteen: "God Never Wastes Pain"

Myth: God doesn't seem good to let you suffer. What a waste.
Fact: God never wastes pain. He uses it to conform us into the image of His Son, which is the best possible outcome for anyone. "For those God foreknew he also predestined to be conformed to the likeness of his Son, that he might be the firstborn among many brothers" (Romans 8:29, NIV 1984).

Temporary suffering reaps eternal rewards as we let Jesus grow and show through us as we endure. **Take God's Word for it:** "[But what of that?] For I consider that the sufferings of this present time (this present life) are not worth being compared with the glory that is about to be revealed to us and in us and for us and conferred on us!"- Romans 8:18, AMP

Seventeen: How to Avoid Making Problems Worse

It's everywhere -even in small towns. Small businesses offer "healing" services with evil elements covered up by innocent-sounding names like "energy movement" or "Reiki massage". Let's get this straight so that we don't injure our already hurting lives...
Myth: Energy movements or New Age can help your pain.

Truth: New Age means "old lie": the devil deceives patients who desire to get help but instead invite demonic activity via such practices.

With much prayer and sincerity, I warn you: Don't listen to the "light and energy" movement. It's a counterfeit comfort source. Horrible things have happened to people because of it. Also, when discouraged, never turn to a horoscope. I share this to warn you as I would a kid playing on the Autobahn: You'll get hit! The enemy gets a foothold if you hold horoscopes in esteem.

Stay FAR away from horoscopes, games with fortune-telling, psychics, and anything similar. It's like inviting evil into your life.

But Jesus can keep you safe and hold you close! Take God's Word for it: "Be sober, be vigilant; because your adversary the devil, as a roaring lion, walketh about, seeking whom he may devour: Whom resist steadfast in the faith, knowing that the same afflictions are accomplished in your brethren that are in the world. But the God of all grace, who hath called us unto his eternal glory by Christ Jesus, after that ye have suffered a while, make you perfect, stablish, strengthen, settle you. To him be glory and dominion forever and ever. Amen." (See I Peter 5:8-10.)

Eighteen: Be a Courageous Christian

Take God's Word for it: "Speak up for those who cannot speak for themselves; ensure justice for those being crushed."-Proverbs 31:8

"But thanks be to God, who gives us the victory through our Lord Jesus Christ."-I Cor. 15:58

Warning: The application of this devotional requires true devotion to Jesus and His Word in a world hostile to Him. While entirely dependent upon God, we must pray for and stand up for the defenseless. Today, at risk of sounding extreme, I must tell you: A hell-driven attack on human life continues to assail America and other nations. Abortion and passive euthanasia for the elderly continue to snuff out lives in the disguise of compassion. We have seen firsthand the effects on various elderly patients in need of advocates. Passive euthanasia is happening. Often, the elderly, under the guise of compassion, receive less care so they can "die with dignity" or some other excuse...masking passive euthanasia. [Passive euthanasia is when a person dies prematurely because of having all medicines, food, and drink removed when the patient could actually live longer with compassionate care.]

God hates passive euthanasia and abortion. Abortion and passive euthanasia share something in common: They sacrifice lives to the altar of convenience for others. **But God loves the people who sinned in these ways and desires them to come to repentance.** He offers forgiveness and freedom through Jesus! (Click here to learn how to know God and go to Heaven.) Again, it's time to bow down and stand up. We must stand up for those who can't! "Speak up for those who cannot speak for themselves; ensure justice for those being crushed" (Proverbs 31:8). Please pray and share this prayer with other believers.

Let us pray now:

"Heavenly Father, we bow before You and plead for Your mercy to flood our culture and help people to fight for life for the unborn

AND the elderly. Lord God, we need Your help and invite You to fight on their behalf, as You share in Your Word. Please draw families to Yourself and bless the elderly with personal relationships with You. We ask for Your help to help them. In Jesus' Name, Amen."

As we march forward in faith, may we all remember that God preserves the souls of those who die in Christ Jesus! He remains good and will have ultimate victory over evil! So, fellow believers, as we pray for and fight for life, let's remember that we have 100% guaranteed victory in Jesus. Begin to pray for nursing homes in your area. And visit them. And may we not forget the aim of our charge: **"The aim of our charge is love that issues from a pure heart and a good conscience and a sincere faith"** (I Timothy 1:5).

Nineteen: Feel like a Child Again with Your Heavenly Father

"Shauntee" waited in line at graduation. She had befriended her dad on Facebook, and invited him to come see her graduate. It took a flash of bravery for her to click "send" on her message to him. Now, she took a step forward in line for her diploma. Each step pushed her towards where she could see the line-up of parents. Her mom stood there alone. He hadn't shown. And that showed a lot to Shauntee. Tears fell. Yet her Heavenly Father collected every tear.

Another child felt a hurt that lasted into his 90's: Last week, I picked up a memoir of a man in his 90's. "Herb" wrote about his dad and mom. They'd never hugged him. They'd never told him that they loved him. He did everything he could to earn praise. And, even in his 90's, his heart hurt just as much as "Shauntee".

But God never forgets to hug you. He never fails to come. He never runs away. Instead, He opens His arms wide to you. Such love... such acceptance...such grace! Do you know God as Father? When you accept Jesus, God accepts you into His family.

You can feel like a child again by getting a new life, a new birth in Christ!

Guess what? No one is too old to be like a child with the Lord. No one is too old to be born again as a fully adopted child of God! Be like a child and come to Jesus. Jesus said in Matthew 18:3 (AMP), "...Truly I say to you, unless you repent (change, turn about) and become like little children [trusting, lowly, loving, forgiving], you can never enter the kingdom of heaven [at all]." Click here to learn how to know God and go to Heaven.

`Whether you're 19 or 91, it's time to be trusting, lowly, loving, and forgiving as we look to our Heavenly Father. Remember Him on Father's Day each year. Spend time with Him. Be like a child in your complete trust, love, and reliance on Him. And boast about Him to your friends while inviting them to know Him, too. He loves you with an everlasting love and underneath are His everlasting arms!

Take God's Word for It: "See what [an incredible] quality of love the Father has given (shown, bestowed on) us, that we should [be permitted to] be named and called and counted the children of God!"-I John 3:1a

Twenty: Erasing Fear

The worst fear imaginable is being forsaken by God. And He's promised never, ever to do that, my fellow believers. So your worst fear will never happen! Also, remember this: Jesus is coming back and He will make all things right in the end! And He's promised to be with you always. He said so! And He always keeps His Word.

The inspiring Joni Eareckson Tada, who was completely paralyzed after a diving accident, shared a powerful testimony and said it well: "All you really need is the One who promised never to leave or forsake you--the One who said, 'Lo, I am with you always.'"

Yes! It's true! He says to you even in your intense pain, "I am with you always." Now, it's time to soak in God's truth. Let His love wash over you as you drink of the Living Water. What a refreshing splash of His Word is found in this passage:

"Who shall separate us from the love of Christ? Shall tribulation, or distress, or persecution, or famine, or nakedness, or danger, or sword? No, in all these things we are more than conquerors through him who loved us. For I am sure that neither death nor life, nor angels nor rulers, nor things present nor things to come, nor powers, nor height nor depth, nor anything else in all creation, will be able to separate us from the love of God in Christ Jesus our Lord."-Romans 8:35, 37-39

Open up with God and share your heartache. And receive His love and comfort instead of blockading yourself with questions. And then help and pray with someone who has it worse than you. And remember that God will make all things new.

Take God's Word for it: "For, behold, I create new heavens and a new earth: and the former shall not be remembered, nor come into mind" (Isaiah 65:17).

Twenty-One: Jesus *Does* Understand

Do you feel alone and like no one understands? Jesus understands. God's very own Son understands! Think about it: Betrayed? So was He. In pain? His pain exceeded ours. Grieving? He knew grief. Poor? He didn't even have a place to rest His head. Oh, yes, our Savior knows well what it's like to be human. Yet He, being the only Son of God, was sinless, took our punishment, and rose again that we might be saved from hell, where people get punished forever for rejecting God.

Pour out your heart to Him. He poured out His blood for you. Yes, Jesus loves me. Yes, Jesus loves you. Lean on Him -not feelings. He'll carry you. Take God's Word for it: "Therefore he had to be made like his brothers in every respect, so that he might become a merciful and faithful high priest in the service of God, to make propitiation for the sins of the people" (Heb. 2:17).

"Since then we have a great high priest who has passed through the heavens, Jesus, the Son of God, let us hold fast our confession" (Heb. 4:14).

"For we do not have a High Priest Who is unable to understand and sympathize and have a shared feeling with our weaknesses and infirmities and liability to the assaults of temptation, but One Who has been tempted in every respect as we are, yet without sinning" (Heb. 4:15).

Learn of Jesus. And lean on Jesus. Yes, God knows what you're going through. And Jesus never backs away.

Twenty-Two: God's Plans for You Are Good

Take God's Word for It: "For I know the plans I have for you," declares the LORD, "plans to prosper you and not to harm you, plans to give you hope and a future."-Jeremiah 29:11

"If only I had this person on our ministry team..." I remember thinking and praying for a certain person to be a part of our ministry. After a long time, the person joined us and started to work. Well, we thought the person was going to work. Unfortunately, the individual was all Christian talk and no walk.

God taught me much through the experience. He taught me to trust Him and ask for His pick for every area of my life. He's since brought wonderful followers of Christ to help us. And I know He'll continue to do so.

Guess what? God has already planned good things for your life! He *does care.* God sees. He loves every life conceived. No mistakes. Just love. How He loves you! And He's created you on purpose for a purpose: to enjoy His presence (which is the most beautiful, truly awesome blessing of all!), love Him and others, share and obey His protective and freeing truth! In fact, He's mapped your life out with the final destination absolutely better than Hawaii or anywhere on earth.

And He did it before you were born! Wow, how I praise Him! Get a grasp of this: "Your eyes saw my unformed substance, and in Your book all the days [of my life] were written before ever they took shape, when as yet there were none of them" (Psalm 139:16).

When you know Jesus, you're God's all-new creation and masterpiece. With God, you can do the impossible and make an eternal difference! He keeps a record. He knows what you do through and for Him.

When done just for Jesus, no task is too small! And, when you're saved, you're saved. And it's exciting to love back with action the One who loved you before you were born! (Come to Jesus to become an all-new creation and be saved from His condemnation. Click here to learn more.) Fellow believer, He's already planned your life. And His plans always exceed our best!

God made you on purpose for a purpose. God loves you....yes, *you*! He has work for you to do! "We are God's masterpiece. He has created us anew in Christ Jesus, so we can do the good things he planned for us long ago."-Eph. 2:10

Remember: Just lean on the Lord and He'll help you fly above your problems and reside in the shadow of His wings! "Be merciful to me, O God, be merciful to me, for in you my soul takes refuge; in the shadow of your wings I will take refuge, till the storms of destruction pass by" (Ps. 57:1). Let's pray and obey His Word. He'll do the rest! His plans exceed our best!

Twenty-Three: Trade Self-Talk for God-Talk

On March 10th 2012, Nadine Schweigert married herself in Fargo, North Dakota. Yes, it included the dress, flowers, the cake...the everything (including a honeymoon in New Orleans). Her innocent 11 year old son felt sick about it. Here's how she described his reaction: "Initially his response was to put his hand on my shoulder. He said, 'I love you, but I'm embarrassed for you right now and I'm not coming.'" (Let's pray for Nadine, her son, and those who are like her today.)

Think this is an isolated thing? No. An anti-God and pro-self movement exists. And New Age web sites promote self-marriage. This is the devil's way of deceiving people into an eternity of punishment apart from God.

When people buy into doing things the world's way, they sell their souls to pay. Yet, as they're deceived, they receive nothing but evil. It reminds me of the rich man Jesus described in Luke 12: "So he said, 'I will do this: I will pull down my barns and build greater, and there I will store all my crops and my goods. And I will say to my soul, "Soul, you have many goods laid up for many years; take your ease; eat, drink, and be merry."' But God said to him, 'Fool! This night your soul will be required of you; then whose will those things be which you have provided?' "So is he who lays up treasure for himself, and is not rich toward God." (Today, be sure you know that you're saved from sin and death. Be sure to receive God's free gift of salvation in Christ now because we'll all face Him later. Click here to learn more about it!)

Interestingly, in the verses that followed in Luke 12, Jesus then continued to point out about how believers need not worry: "Then He said to His disciples, 'Therefore I say to you, do not worry about your life, what you will eat; nor about the body, what you will put on. Life is more than food, and the body is more than clothing."

Wow, what a contrast! We believers don't even have to worry! So are you a believer who, although storing treasure in Heaven, is losing joy as you worry? (Been there.) Well, here are some tips to help us all:

Tips for a Believer's Recovery from a Bout of Worry:

- Replace self-talk with God talk! Instead of a worried daze, decide to pray and praise! God made you on purpose for a purpose and nothing compares to enjoying Him! "Heal me, O Lord, and I shall be healed; Save me, and I shall be saved, For You are my praise" (Jeremiah 17:14).
- Read Scripture out loud and listen to an audio Bible.
- Realize you're not odd. You're God's! You're not a mistake. God never makes mistakes! So remove items that promote a worldly me-centeredness and replace them with items

to promote a Christ-centeredness. Add Christian decor to your home.

- Listen, then glisten! Listen to God and you'll glisten while rejoicing in Him! Spend time listening to God's voice. Be still and listen to Him. How? Read His Word and let His Holy Spirit guide you.

- Worry exits when worship enters. When you worship God, you won't look at the earth stuff and worry. Praise God more and worry less. Keep a journal of praise to God! Here's a start: I praise You, Lord! My heart sings to Yours! You alone deserve all worship and praise all of my days! "Sing to the LORD, bless His name; Proclaim the good news of His salvation from day to day."-Psalm 96:2

Do not worry. Beautiful reminder, isn't it? Worry reflects a focus on self and a distrust of God. Believe God and store up treasures in Heaven! "Do not lay up for yourselves treasures on earth, where moth and rust destroy and where thieves break in and steal; but lay up for yourselves treasures in heaven, where neither moth nor rust destroys and where thieves do not break in and steal" (Matthew 6:19-20).

Twenty-Four: More Tips to Recharge with God

Be willing. We must be willing, and doing God's will is thrilling! God provides amazing opportunities to serve Him. Never underestimate God. God provides amazing opportunities to serve Him. He can use anyone willing to follow and obey. Simply bow before the Lord and say, "Please use me. I'm willing!" Copy and paste Isaiah 6:8 onto your heart: "Also I heard the voice of the Lord, saying, Whom shall I send? And who will go for Us? Then said I, Here am I; send me" (Is. 6:8).

It may feel impossible to pray, but pray anyway. In Luke 18:27, Jesus said, "What is impossible with men is possible with God." Regardless of what our natural, foggy perspective might be, we must pray anyway. **Things can look bad, but God remains good!** So let's pray without ceasing! And always ask that God's will -not ours- be done. Be willing to trade my for Thy. "Thy will be done." Today's devotional features God's Word (as usual!) and a personal story.

It seemed impossible, but I prayed with the lady anyway: At an important event, a lady needed to visit with a leader who could really help her mission. I offered to pray with her, and we prayed on the spot. As we lifted our heads and said, "Amen," the leader rounded the corner! And, lo and behold, he started to visit with her! God did it! He allowed them to meet and the leader has helped her mission immensely! God receives all glory! His light cannot be stopped by dark situations!

In a dark time that seems "impossible"? Look up to Jesus! He's the ever-brilliant King of kings! I love this Scripture and must share it with you: "Which [appearing] will be shown forth in His own proper time by the blessed, only Sovereign (Ruler), the King of kings and the Lord of lords, Who alone has immortality [in the sense of exemption from every kind of death] and lives in unapproachable light, Whom no man has ever seen or can see. Unto Him be honor and everlasting power and dominion. Amen (so be it)" (I Tim. 6:15-16).

Today, as with the lady at the event, it may feel impossible to pray. But pray anyway. God's answer could be on the way! Fellow believers, remember: No matter what happens, Romans 8:28 will happen! (Learn how to know God on a personal level and be sure you'll go to Heaven when you die. If using the e-book, click here.)

For the lady at the event, it seemed impossible. But we prayed anyway and God answered even while we prayed! Now, this encouraged me because I've prayed for years about certain things and not seen the answer round the corner immediately. Sometimes, His answers baffle me. But, praise God, He is sovereign! No matter how He answers and when, He does it out of His love.

God's love overwhelms me! Wow, how He loves you! How He loves me! Because of His love, Jesus came: "Because of and in order to satisfy the great and wonderful and intense love with which He loved us..." (Excerpt from Eph. 2:3, AMP.)

In conclusion, enjoy God's Word as the final word for this devotional (and for life): "And therefore the Lord [earnestly] waits [expecting, looking, and longing] to be gracious to you; and therefore He lifts Himself up, that He may have mercy on you and show loving-kindness to you. For the Lord is a God of justice. Blessed (happy, fortunate, to be envied) are all those who [earnestly] wait for Him, who expect and look and long for Him [for His victory, His favor, His love, His peace, His joy, and His matchless, unbroken companionship]!"-**Isaiah 30:18**

Prayer Tip of the Week: Pray with someone over your noon hour. Use the phone, if necessary. I Thess. 5:17 includes an amazing reminder: "Be unceasing in prayer [praying perseveringly]..."

Twenty-Five: Embrace your identity in Christ

When I've dealt with event security people or the Secret Service, I've experienced no problems. They allow me backstage because I'm part of the program. A background check, I.D. check, etc. may occur beforehand. Whether sharing or singing, I've been backstage all kinds of places -ranging from President George W. Bush's venue to Fox News in NYC.

Stacie and Carrie's album, In God We Still Trust

One time, I did encounter a problem. A rude remark from a security guard caught me off-guard. He blocked Carrie's and my entry. But he couldn't take away the truth: We were already in the program.

Today, someone might rudely try to steal your focus from your true identity: Someone's rude words, actions, or insinuations can hurt and distract us from our true identity in Christ. It's difficult.

Not familiar with what I mean? Well, people trade their old ID of "lost sinner" for "found family member" when they're born again. God can make you all-new and cleanse you from every mistake (sin) if you believe, repent, and receive Jesus as your personal Savior and Lord!

Get your ID from Christ. Fellow followers of Jesus, don't let fellow human beings (including yourself) determine your identity. Yes, fellow believers, He adopted you. Just think of it and praise Him for it! To quote from I John 3:2, "Beloved, we are God's children now..." That's all that counts! You belong to the highest kingdom without end. How amazingly gracious is He!! Read and prayerfully apply Scripture to your heart. Here are some ways to do this:

- *Keep a list of Scriptures that apply to your own particular past labelings and grasp Christ's truths for you instead.*
- *Example: If you were rejected, memorize a verse like Acts 15:8:*

"God, who knows the heart, showed that he accepted them by giving the Holy Spirit to them, just as he did to us."

- *If insulted by someone, find a verse that applies to your situation.*
- *Print off these verses about it:*
- *Remember this: "But you are a chosen race, a royal priesthood, a dedicated nation, [God's] own purchased, special people, that you may set forth the wonderful deeds and display the virtues and perfections of Him Who called you out of darkness into His marvelous light."-I Peter 2:9 (AMP)*
- *Soak in the truth: "[We pray] that you may be invigorated and strengthened with all power according to the might of His glory, [to exercise] every kind of endurance and patience (perseverance and forbearance) with joy, Giving thanks to the Father, Who has qualified and made us fit to share the portion which is the inheritance of the saints (God's holy people) in the Light. [The Father] has delivered and drawn us to Himself out of the control and the dominion of darkness and has transferred us into the kingdom of the Son of His love, In Whom we have our redemption through His blood, [which means] the forgiveness of our sins." -I Corinthians 1:11-14*

The next time when you look at your driver's license in your wallet, remember to thank God that your real ID is found in Christ. And be on the lookout for lost people. Share how to be made right and reconciled with God!

Twenty-Six: Child-like Faith and Father-focused Praise!

Employ child-like faith. Cherish and embrace child-like faith.. not childish selfishness. Trust God completely as a little child depends on parents. Believe God. Take Him at His Word and trust Him to take care of everything -even if you understand nothing. Ask Him for help to do this. "But Jesus called them [the parents] to Him, saying, Allow the little children to come to Me, and do not hinder them, for to such [as these] belongs the kingdom of God" (Luke 18:16, AMP).

Enjoy Father-focused praise! Praise God for Who He is -not just what He does!

To get started, here's a quote from my time of praising God: Every bit of glory goes to You, Heavenly Father! No one -no one!- compares to You! We praise and proclaim Jesus Christ! "For what we proclaim is not ourselves, but Jesus Christ as Lord, with ourselves as your servants for Jesus' sake. For God, who said, 'Let light shine out of darkness,' has shone in our hearts to give the light of the knowledge of the glory of God in the face of Jesus Christ. But we have this treasure in jars of clay, to show that the surpassing power belongs to God and not to us"-II Corinthians 4:5-7 (ESV).

Twenty-Seven: From Being "Christian in Name Only" to Beaming His Name Only!

Shallowness filled an expensive meeting room. In an attempt to make the occasion appear noble, a tagline of "Christian" accompanied the event. High-pitched laughter, society hugs, ostentatious and immodest clothes, and jealous glances hid sad, empty hearts. The attendees were Christian in name-only.

In another room with meager decor, Christ's deep, loving presence reigned. People felt truly loved, blessed, and encouraged. Jesus' light shimmered in their eyes, modest apparel, real laughter and joy, and genuine heartfelt expressions prevailed. The attendees proclaimed His Name only.

Plenty of folks put a sticker of "Christian" to their lapels, cars, and events. But we're to know believers by their fruits -not by their self-labels. "Therefore, you will fully know them by their fruits" (Matt. 7:20). "Examine and test and evaluate your own selves to see whether you are holding to your faith and showing the proper fruits of it. Test and prove yourselves [not Christ]. Do you not yourselves realize and know [thoroughly by an ever-increasing experience] that Jesus

Christ is in you--unless you are [counterfeits] disapproved on trial and rejected?" (2 Cor. 13:5, AMP).

Hey, it takes more than a grocery store label to make a fruit. If you see a piece of firewood labeled as "Red Delicious" at the store, you don't buy and eat it. Right?

I've met the richest people whom the world overlooks as "poor."

Some events and attendees are Christian in "name-only." Fellow followers of Jesus, may our sincere love and words proclaim His Name only today and always!

Proclaim His Name only. How? Ask the Holy Spirit to fill you afresh and help you. He'll help you love sincerely, toss aside evil, and hold fast to what is good. "[Let your] love be sincere (a real thing); hate what is evil [loathe all ungodliness, turn in horror from wickedness], but hold fast to that which is good."-Romans 12:9 "Love does no wrong to one's neighbor [it never hurts anybody]. Therefore love meets all the requirements and is the fulfilling of the Law." -Romans 13:10

Prayer Tip: Ask the Holy Spirit to help you so that you can be used to help others.

Week Twenty-Eight: Daily. Living. Worship.

Some churches put pressure to outwardly express worship to God. Some encourage complete containment of outward expression. But what does God desire? He desires us to style our life to worship -not to focus on worship styles.

I read something stated by Billy Graham that encapsulates much about what's important: "Worship in the truest sense takes place only when our full attention is on God - on His glory, power, majesty, love and compassion." This tip could easily fill an entire book. Seriously, sometimes all we need is a gentle reminder to relish in God's rich truth about worship.

No matter where you've been, you can know that Jesus still loves you and His arms remain open! In John 4, we discover a woman with a shockingly immoral past. Yet Jesus didn't just talk about her and her habitual sin. He told her the truth and how to win through Him!

That is true for you, too: Come to Jesus. He's the only Way to Heaven. Through life in Him, true worship takes place. But you have to be made right with God first. God can make you all-new and cleanse you from every mistake (sin) if you believe, repent, and receive Jesus as your personal Savior and Lord!

Now, back to focusing on John 4. In it, Jesus said something about worship that we all should heed: "God is spirit, and those who worship him must worship in spirit and truth" (John 4:34). Here are a few ways to do this:

- *Don't depend on a person to prompt you to worship. Depend on the Holy Spirit.*
- *Praise God by praying the Psalms! This remains an amazing way to integrate God's Word and personally relish in His infinitely awesome presence!!*
- *Daily. Make it a daily experience to worship from your heart in response to His.*
- *Living. Live a life of holiness which gives glory to God. Live in Christ. He alone makes us alive after being dead in our trespasses.*
- *Worship. Worship with music can be great. But the main aspect is to uninhibitedly worship God in spirit and truth -not in hand movements and hypocrisy.*

Do things in worship to God: Walk in the Spirit. Walk in truth. When you do, you'll walk in daily, living worship! Daily. Living. Worship. "But I say, walk and live [habitually] in the [Holy] Spirit [responsive to and controlled and guided by the Spirit]; then you will certainly not gratify the cravings and desires of the flesh (of human nature without God)" (Galatians 5:16, AMP). "Teach me Your way, O Lord, that I may walk and live in Your truth; direct and unite my heart [solely, reverently] to fear and honor Your name" (Psalm 86:11).

Prayer Tip: Ask the Holy Spirit to help you worship more and worry less!

Twenty-Nine: The Truth about Love: Yes! God still loves *you*.

Newsflash: You can't earn God's love. He already loves you! Let His love flood and overflow through you. 1 John 4:11 says it well, "Beloved, if God loved us so [very much], we also ought to love one another."

You don't have to be gorgeous, rich, or famous. He loves you as you are and He desires you to desire Him most. How He loves you, my friend! Let Jesus hold you and carry you. Release your worries and embrace your Savior. Believe. Repent. Receive. He is Lord. Oh, the deep, deep love of Jesus! And guess what? You can be yourself with Him.

Pour your heart out to your Lord. Be yourself with Him. Be yourself, my fellow follower of Jesus. He already knows you and loves you. "Trust in, lean on, rely on, and have confidence in Him at all times, you people; pour out your hearts before Him. God is a refuge for us (a fortress and a high tower). Selah [pause, and calmly think of that]!"-Ps. 62:8

As Dr. Adrian Rogers said, "Lust wants to get. Love wants to give!" Some people mislabel sin and call it "love" while abusing and excusing their way through life. They can call it "just the way it is now" or whatever. But if God calls it a sin, it's a sin. Let's repent and turn to God, who loves us and wants what's best for us! Today is the day to turn and return to God! There is hope in Jesus!

God's love never abuses you. Some people -even in the disguise of Christian language- do hateful things and pretend it's with God's love. But I Corinthians 13 remains the love standard. And God loves us perfectly! Read this like you've never read it before: "For God so greatly loved and dearly prized the world that He [even] gave up His only begotten (unique) Son, so that whoever believes in (trusts in, clings to, relies on) Him shall not perish (come to destruction, be lost) but have eternal (everlasting) life" (John 3:16).

Believe the truth about love…Yes! God still loves *you*. *Let His love flood you and overflow into others' lives.* Oh, how God loves you! The immensity of God's love for us infinitely surpasses our best efforts to comprehend it. Beyond our brains' capacities, God's love cannot be contained by a writer's best words or a speaker's best speech. The infinite immensity of God's love continues for you now. Do you know Jesus as your personal Savior and Lord of your life? If so, you can call out to God as your Father! Take God's Word for it: **"How great is the love the Father has lavished on us, that we should be called children of God! And that is what we are! The reason the world does not know us is that it did not know him"** (I John 1:3).

Thirty: It's Time for Church Take-Out!

One day, I waited in an empty room for an appointment with someone. I looked up at the fluorescent light in the ceiling and it hit me: (The light didn't hit me. A light bulb went off in my head. Just had to clarify!) Seriously, here's what I realized: We need to get back to the "Greats." What do I mean? The Greatest Commandments and the Great Commission. Have you considered the "Greats" in God's Word?

Many churches today think we need to copy the world to reach it. But it's the opposite: Copy the Word and God will reach the world.

Outreach is to reach out…not in. It's not about "What do I get out of church?" It's about "How do I take church out to the world?" We need to be enjoying Jesus in church and then taking it out to the world.

When I'm at a restaurant, the portions overwhelm me. Just ask people close to me: I usually clutch a take-out box when exiting the eatery. **That's the way it needs to be at church: Feed on God's Word and then take It out to the world!**

Last Sunday, I heard God's Word at church. (This alone remains something to treasure. So many countries attempt to muzzle

Christians!) I savored the Holy Spirit's guidance of the guest speaker. Amongst other amazing insights, he spoke about the way God is moving in different countries and the need for revival in America. Have you prayed for revival today?

Today let's pray and obey the "Greats."

The Greatest Commandments:
"And one of their number, a lawyer, asked Him a question to test Him. Teacher, which kind of commandment is great and important (the principal kind) in the Law? [Some commandments are light--which are heavy?] And He replied to him, You shall love the Lord your God with all your heart and with all your soul and with all your mind (intellect).This is the great (most important, principal) and first commandment. And a second is like it: You shall love your neighbor as [you do] yourself. These two commandments sum up and upon them depend all the Law and the Prophets." -Matthew 22:35-40 (Amplified Bible)

The Great Commission:
"Afterward He appeared to the Eleven [apostles themselves] as they reclined at table; and He reproved and reproached them for their unbelief (their lack of faith) and their hardness of heart, because they had refused to believe those who had seen Him and looked at Him attentively after He had risen [from death]. And He said to them, Go into all the world and preach and publish openly the good news (the Gospel) to every creature [of the whole human race]. "-Mark 16:14-16, AMP

Thirty-One: *Act like you believe Whom you believe.*

Have you ever had such a bad start to the week that you wish it could fast-forward to the weekend? Well, at the time of writing this devotional, I've had quite a week! When one bad thing happened, another bad thing quickly followed. Gulp. Nothing life-threatening happened. But it simply didn't go smoothly. Some weeks can take the wind out of our sails and sink the boat, too. But remember, fellow believers, Jesus walked on water and He's promised to carry us through: Yes! We have Jesus! Jesus empowers believers to overcome the world!

"I have told you these things, so that in Me you may have [perfect] peace and confidence. In the world you have tribulation and trials and distress and frustration; but be of good cheer [take courage; be confident, certain, undaunted]! For I have overcome the world. [I have deprived it of power to harm you and have conquered it for you.]"
-Jesus, as quoted in John 16:33

Today, I challenge myself and all of us to look to Jesus. *It's time to act like we believe Whom we believe! And it's time to remember that, yes, Jesus IS coming again!*

God always wins! So let's focus on Him and worship Jesus. That's how the disciples responded when they saw the risen Jesus. The only correct response to Jesus is pure, passionate worship!

Worthy is the Lamb! Let's return to a focus on His return! Let's read this aloud together:

"He who testifies to these things says,
'Surely I am coming quickly.'
Amen. Even so, come, Lord Jesus!"
-Rev. 22:20

About the Authors:

Stacie Ruth Stoelting writes, speaks, and sings to give glory to God and to share the truth of His love with others. Having written a book at age fifteen, she possesses a uniquely urgent passion for sharing Jesus with the lost and the hurting. She invites you to join her prayer group at www.PrayingPals.org.

Carrie Beth Stoelting enjoys political activism, desires to do what's right, and sings to her Lord and Savior, Jesus Christ. She also has a site for cleaning up Hollywood: www.unitedformovieaction.com.

Both sisters have sung for national leaders, shared on Fox News and other major news outlets, and reached out to veterans –particularly after they witnessed a fatal accident and learned a tiny bit of the violence witnessed by veterans. They hope in Jesus and pray you'll join them as they follow Him. He is for real! Learn more at www. BrightLightMinistries.com.

Bibliography

New American Standard Bible. (1995). La Habra, California: The Lockman Foundation.

Social Darwinism. (2013). Retrieved from Merriam-Webster.com: http://unabridged.merriam-webster.com/collegiate/social%20Darwinism

Barton, D. (2012). *America's Most Biblically-Hostile U. S. President.* Aledo, Texas: Wallbuilders.

Bradford, M. (1994). *Founding Fathers: Brief Lives of the Framers of the United States Constitution.* University of Kansas Press.

Bradford, M. (1993). *Original Intentions: On the Making and Ratification of the United States Constitution.* University of Georgia Press.

Christians victims of rising 'hostility' from gov't and secular groups, report says. (2012, August 26). Retrieved 26 2012, August, from FoxNews.com: http://www.foxnews.com/us/2012/08/24/christians-victims-rising-hostility-from-govt-and-secular-groups-report-says/

Clinton, T., & Ohlschlager, G. (2002). *Competant Christian counseling, Volume One.* Colorado Springs: WaterBrook Press.

Congress, U. C. (1774-1788). *Journals of the American Congress From 1774 to 1788.* Washington, D.C.: Way and Gideon.

Constitutional Convention . (1787). *U.S. Constitution.*

Continental Congress. (1776). *Declaration of Independence.*

DeMoss, N. L. (2011, May 4). *Brokenness Bookmark.* Retrieved September 8, 2012, from www.ReviveOurHearts.com: http://www.reviveourhearts.com/articles/brokenness-bookmark-the-heart-god-revives/

DeMoss, N. L. (2005). *Brokenness Bookmark: The Heart God Revives.* Moody Publishers.

Dreisbach, D. (2006). Origins and Dangers of the 'Wall of Separation' Between Church and State. *Imprimis (a publication of Hillsdale College).*

Eggerichs, E. (2004). *Love and Respect.* Nashville, TN: Thomas Nelson.

Find Your Representative. (n.d.). Retrieved from https://writerep. house.gov/writerep/welcome.shtml

Focus on the Family. (2011). *Founding Faith: Christians in America.* Colorado Springs: Focus on the Family.

FoxNews.com. (2012, August 26). Christians victims of rising 'hostility' from gov't and secular groups, report says. *FoxNews.com* , pp. 1-3.

FRC. (2012). *2012 Values Voter Presidential Voter Guide.* Retrieved from http://downloads.frcaction.org/EF/EF11L04.pdf

Hamilton, Alexander. J. M. (1787-1788). *Federalist Papers.*

Kassian, M. (2005). *The Feminist Mistake.* Wheaton: Crossway.

Kassian, M. (2010). *Girls Gone Wise.* Chicago: Moody Publishers.

Kersten, K. (1994). How the feminist establishment hurts women: A Christian critique of a movement gone wrong. *Christianity Today.*

King, H. T. (1997). *Fresh Encounter.* Broadman & Holman.

Liberty Institute. (2012). *The Survey of Religious Hostility in America.* Washington, D.C.: Family Research Council.

McCulley, C. (2008). *Radical Womanhood: Feminine Faith in a Feminist World*. Chicago: Moody Publishers.

National Association of Pro-life Nurses. (n.d.). Retrieved from http://www.nursesforlife.org/

Nicholson, A. (1854). *Reports of the Committees of the House of Representatives Made During the First Session of the Thirty-Third Congress*. Washington.

Madison, J. (1789). *Bill of Rights*.

(n.d.). Retrieved from AMillionThanks.org: www.amillionthanks.org

(n.d.). Retrieved from WallBuilders.com: www.wallbuilders.com

Sanger, M. (1918). *Morality and Birth Control*, 11, 14.

Santorum, R. (2006). *It Takes a Family: Conservatism and the Common Good* . Wilmington: Intercollegiate Studies Institute.

Schlafly, P., & Venker, S. (2011). *The Flipside of Feminism: What Conservative Women Know — and Men Can't Say*. Torrance: WND.

Spilka, B., & Ladd, K. L. (2012). *The Psychology of Prayer: A Scientific Approach*. New York, NY: The Guilford Press.

Stoelting, S. a. (n.d.). *Know God*. Retrieved from Praying Pals: http://prayingpals.org/knowgod.html

The Star Spangled Banner. (2011, June 1). Retrieved 2012, from Conservapedia: http://conservapedia.com/Pledge_of_Allegiance

Wallbuilders. (2012). *Are You Registered?* . Retrieved from http://www.wallbuilders.com/vote/

Washington, G. (1789). *First Inaugural Address*.

Wilhoit, J. C. (1995). *Nurture That Is Christian*. Grand Rapids: Baker Books.